MAKING MATHEMATICS

A Secondary Course

4

Second Edition—Metric

D. PALING
C. S. BANWELL
K. D. SAUNDERS

OXFORD UNIVERSITY PRESS
1971

Oxford University Press, Ely House, London W.1

GLASGOW NEW YORK TORONTO MELBOURNE WELLINGTON
CAPE TOWN SALISBURY IBADAN NAIROBI LUSAKA ADDIS ABABA
BOMBAY CALCUTTA MADRAS KARACHI LAHORE DACCA
KUALA LUMPUR SINGAPORE HONG KONG TOKYO

MAKING MATHEMATICS

This series is planned to cover a five-year course. Books 1, 2, and 3, together with a Workbook for each, provide material for the first three years. Book 4 and a Workbook, together with twelve or more Topic books, covers the work of the fourth and fifth years. The whole series is designed to provide a balanced course based on class, group, and individual activities.

Note (1) It is suggested that only the first part of each section in Book 4 should be covered on the first reading.

    (2) Most of the Topic books can be used at any time during the fourth and fifth years. They are not directly dependent on Book 4.

PHOTOTYPESET BY BAS PRINTERS LIMITED, WALLOP, HAMPSHIRE
PRINTED IN GREAT BRITAIN BY
WILLIAM CLOWES AND SONS LTD., LONDON AND BECCLES

CONTENTS

TWO-STATE SYSTEMS

For discussion

Use Worksheet 1.
Start at the arrow and with your finger trace a route through the maze to one of the exits **A, B, C, D** and **E**. (You must not turn back at any stage.)

At each junction you have a choice of turning left or right and you can describe your path in terms of *lefts* and *rights*.
For example, trace this path through the maze: *left, left, right, left*.
At which exit do you arrive?

Using *lefts* and *rights* give a route to exit **D**. Now give another route to **D**.
Give a route to: (a) exit **A**; (b) exit **E**; (c) exit **C**.

An experiment

It is advisable to work with a partner for this activity.
You need a coin and Worksheet 2.

The idea is to use the coin to decide which route is taken through the maze.
Start at the arrow. Toss the coin. See whether it is a *head* or a *tail*

If it is a *head* go to the *left*
at the first junction.

If it is a *tail* go to the *right*
at the first junction.

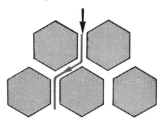 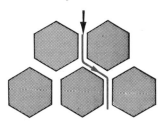

Toss the coin again.
If it is a *head* go *left* at the second junction. If it is a *tail* go *right*.
Do this twice more until you arrive at one of the exits.
At which exit did you arrive?
Record this on a table, as shown,
by putting a stroke in the correct
row.
Repeat this activity until you have
made 48 routes through the maze.

A	
B	
C	
D	
E	

Look at your table of results.
At which exit or exits have most routes arrived?
Can you suggest a reason for this?
At which exit or exits have fewest routes arrived?
Can you suggest a reason for this?

Now put together the results of the whole class and show them in a table,
like this:

Exit	A	B	C	D	E
Number of routes arriving at exit					

Draw a graph of these results.
Keep your tables and graph, you will need them later.

For discussion

Look at the maze at the top of the opposite page.
The exits are labelled **A, B, C, D** and **E** as before.
The junctions within the maze are now also labelled.

Starting at the arrow follow the route *Left, Right, Left, (LRL)*
Have you arrived at **G**?

Record this route as: **G** *(LRL)*

Find a different route to **G** and record it in a similar way.

Find all the different routes to **G** and record them.
What do you notice about the letters in these routes?

Do you agree that there are 3 different routes to **G**?
Record this fact, using Worksheet 3, by writing a 3 above the **G**, as shown on
the lower maze on the opposite page.

In the same way find and record the number of different routes to the other
junctions in the maze and also to the exits.

Look carefully at your *L*s and *R*s for the different routes to each junction
(and each exit).
What do you notice?

Suppose the maze contained another row of hexagons (Worksheet 4).
Can you see a quick way of finding the number of different routes to each of the
new exits?
Copy the numbers from Worksheet 3 and write in the next row.

Can you see how to write more and more rows in this pattern of numbers?

This pattern of numbers is known as Pascal's triangle.
It is named after the French mathematician Pascal who lived in the
seventeenth century.
The pattern is of considerable importance in mathematics.
We shall find out more about it later.

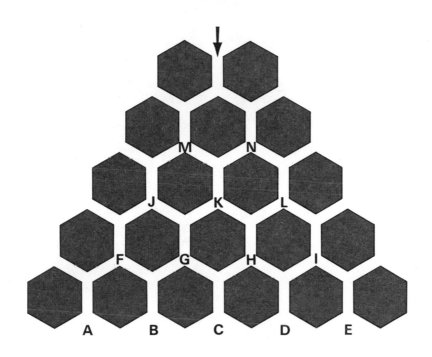

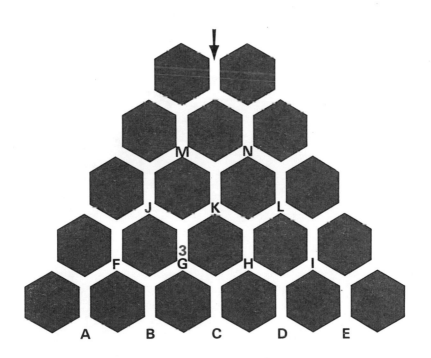

Blaise Pascal

Blaise Pascal was born in France in 1623. He died in 1662 at the early age of 39. His father was an important government official who believed in educating his children at home, and thought that mathematics should not be studied until the age of 16.

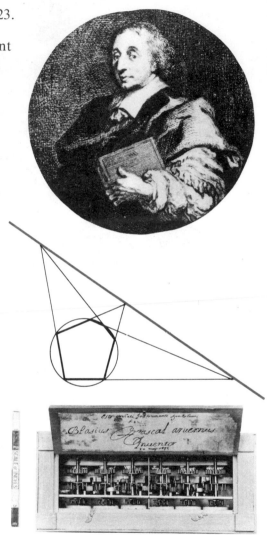

However, Blaise secretly studied mathematics before this age, drawing geometric diagrams on the floor of his room. Working on his own he soon mastered much of the mathematics of that time. His father, eventually discovering his son's brilliance at the subject, bought him mathematical books.

At the age of 16 Blaise Pascal discovered a new theorem concerning a hexagon drawn in a circle. An article which he wrote about this theorem earned him praise from the mathematicians of the day.

Through helping his father with long and tedious calculations, Blaise became interested in developing a calculating device; and at 18 he had designed the first machine that could add, subtract, multiply and divide. Its interior is shown in the photograph.

Soon after this, however, Blaise Pascal became fanatically religious and studied mathematics only when his interest in religion occasionally lapsed. During one of these lapses, while playing a gambling game with dice, he became interested in probability. With another mathematician, Fermat, he developed the use of his 'triangle' of numbers for calculating probabilities in games, heredity, and many other events.

Theory and practice

For discussion

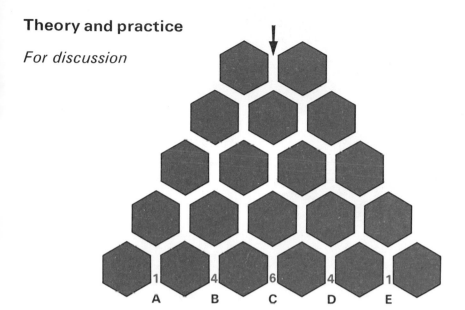

Look at your hexagon maze on Worksheet 3.
Do you agree that the number of routes to the exits **A**, **B**, **C**, **D** and **E** are as
shown on the maze above?

Can you now see why, in your experiment with the coin, most routes arrived at
C, and least routes arrived at **A** or **E**?

The total number of different routes to the exits is 16 (i.e. $1+4+6+4+1$).
Only one of these goes to **A**. So, in theory, only 1 out of every 16 should
finish at **A**.

Look at your table of results for the experiment. Calculate the total number
of routes used in the experiment. Now calculate $\frac{1}{16}$ of this total.
This is the theoretical number of routes to **A** for your experiment.
Compare this with your actual result.

The number of routes to **D** is 4. So, in theory, 4 out of every 16 (or 1 in 4)
should finish at **D**.
Calculate $\frac{1}{4}$ of the total number of routes used in the experiment. Compare this
with your actual result for **D**.

Repeat this for exits **C**, **E** and **B**.
Draw a graph of the theoretical results of your experiment and compare it
with your graph for the experimental results.

9

A boy or a girl?

For discussion

When you are married how many children would you like to have?
How many *boys*? How many *girls*?

If you have four children, which of the following do you think is most likely?
all *boys*? all *girls*? 3 *boys* and 1 *girl*? 3 *girls* and 1 *boy*? 2 *boys* and 2 *girls*?

In England and Wales together almost a million children are born each year.
Of these the numbers of *boys* and *girls* are about the same (with slightly more
boys than *girls*). So the chance of having a *boy* is about the same as that of
having a *girl*.

The diagrams show the possibilities
for (a)   the first child
     (b)   the first two children.

Can you see why they are
drawn as they are?
Do they remind you of
the hexagon maze?
Can you explain why **BB, BG,
GB** and **GG** are written in
the positions shown?

In a family of two children
what do you think is the
chance that they are:
        (a)   2 *boys*? (b) 2 *girls*?
        (c)   a *boy* and a *girl*
                (not worrying about
                the order of them)?

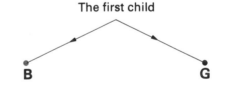

The first child

B   G

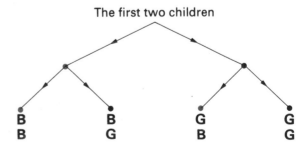

The first two children

B   B   G   G
B   G   B   G

The first four children

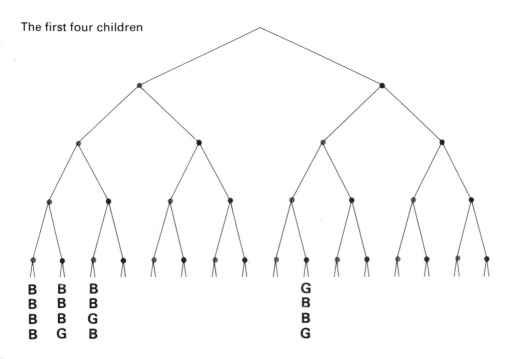

B B B   G
B B B   B
B B G   B
B G B   G

The diagram shows the various possibilities for the first four children.
Complete it (Worksheet 5).

How many different 'routes' are there for the four children?
How many of these give 4 *boys*?
What would you say is the chance of the four children being all *boys*?

How many of the routes give 3 *boys* and 1 *girl*?
What is the chance of having 3 *boys* and 1 *girl* in a family of 4 children (not
worrying about the order in which they are born)?
What is the chance of having: (a) 1 *boy* and 3 *girls*? (b) 2 *boys* and 2 *girls*?

Exercises

1. Use the diagram to find, for a family of 3 children, the chance of having:
   (a) 3 *boys;*   (b) 2 *boys* and 1 *girl;*   (c) 1 *boy* and 2 *girls;*   (d) 3 *girls.*

2. In a family of 5 children what is the chance of having:
   (a) 2 *boys* and 3 *girls*?   (b) 5 *girls*?   (c) 1 *boy* and 4 *girls*?
   Worksheet 6 can be used if necessary.

11

A shunting yard

Look at the drawing on the right of a shunting yard.
At each junction in the network of lines a truck
can be sent to the *left* or to the *right*.

Using *L* for *left* and *R* for *right*
describe the route of a truck which has
to go to:
(a) terminal **G**; (b) terminal **C**.

A coding system can be used to describe
the routes to the various terminals.
This code uses a 0 and a 1

To direct a truck to **C**
the code number is 010 (*LRL*).
To direct a truck to **G** the code
number is 110 (*RRL*).

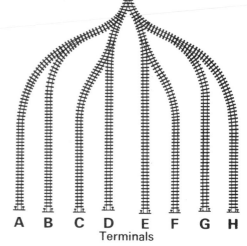

Can you see how this coding system works?
Write the code number for each terminal.

Treat each of these code numbers as a binary (base two) number and change it
to a base ten number. What do you notice?

When a baby is born it is a *boy* or a *girl*. In a maze or in a shunting yard a
left or *right* turn is made. When a coin is tossed it is a *head* or a *tail*.

Each of these is known as a two-state system. Can you see why?

Mr and Mrs John O'Donoghue of Belfields, Australia, with nine of their ten daughters. The tenth and youngest is not shown. The odds against ten children all being girls are 1023 to 1.

Mr and Mrs Emory Harrison of Tennessee, U.S.A., with their thirteen sons. The odds against thirteen children all being boys are 8191 to 1.

PYTHAGORAS

For discussion

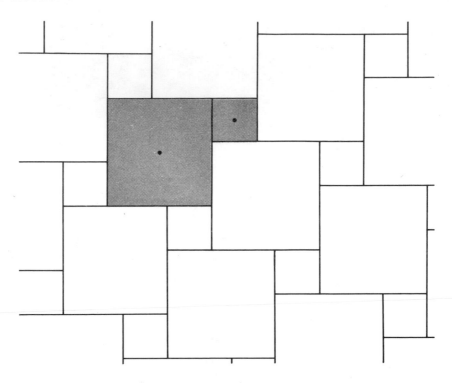

Look at the tiling pattern above.
How do you think the pattern has been made?
Describe the way in which the small squares have been arranged.

Look at the coloured part.
If this is rotated through 90° about the centre of the large square, where can the small square go?
If it is rotated through 90° about the centre of the small square, where can the large square go?

On a large sheet of paper make a pattern like this.
Make your squares larger than those above.
Try *not* to make the side of the smaller square a half (or any other simple fraction) of the side of the larger square.

14   Keep your pattern.

For discussion

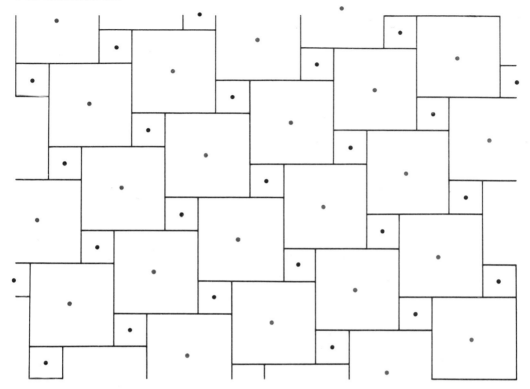

On this pattern the centres of the squares are marked.
What do you notice about: (a) the coloured centres? (b) the black centres?

Use Worksheet 7.
Mark the centres of the large squares in one colour (red).
Mark the centres of the small squares in another colour (green).
Join the red marks to make squares.
Join the green marks to make squares.
What do you notice?

Use your own tiling pattern (or Worksheet 8).
By joining vertices (corners) of the squares draw as many different sized
squares as you can.
Which is the smallest square you can draw? Which is the next smallest?
And the next?

Try to decide on a way of finding the areas of some of your squares.

15

For discussion

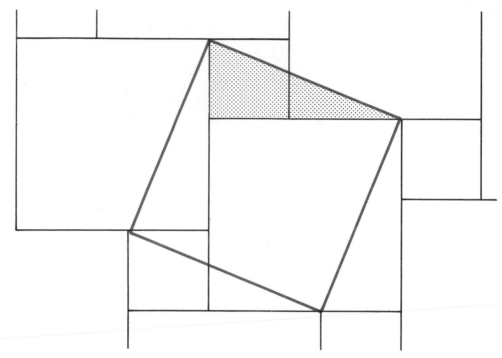

This is part of the pattern you have been looking at.
Draw the coloured square on Worksheet 9.
Cut it out and stick it on a piece of card of the same size.
Check that it fits on the coloured square above.

This cut-out square will have lines on
it, as shown.
Cut along these lines to obtain five
separate pieces.
Reform these pieces to make two squares.
What do you notice about these squares?

What can you say about the areas of the
two squares and the area of the
coloured square?

Look at the shaded triangle at the top
of the page. What can you say about the

16 lengths of its sides?

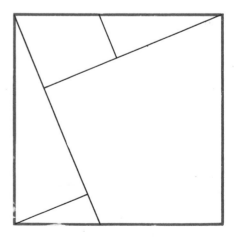

For discussion

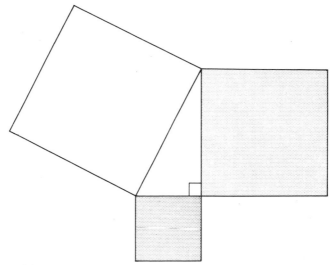

Use Worksheet 10.
Shade the two smaller squares as shown above.

Cut out the two shaded squares, stick on
card, and place them as shown.
Measure the total length along the
bottom of the two squares.
Use this measurement to mark a point *P*,
halfway along the bottom.
Measure the same distance along the
other sides of the large square to get
points like *Q*, *R* and *S*.

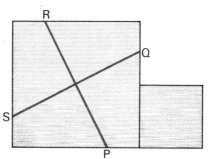

Join these points, as shown, using a coloured pencil.

Cut along the coloured lines.
You should now have five pieces, including the small shaded square.
Arrange the five pieces to form one square.
What can you say about the size of this square?

Repeat this activity for the squares on the sides of the right-angled triangle on
Worksheet 11.

Write a statement about the areas of the squares drawn on the three sides of a
right-angled triangle.

17

2

Pythagoras

Pythagoras was one of the most famous
mathematicians of ancient times.
He lived in the period between 600
and 500 years before Christ.
It is thought that he was born on
the island of Samos and that, after
travelling to many countries, he
settled at Crotona (Crotone), a town
on the south-eastern coast of Italy.
If you find these places on a map you
will see that this was a considerable
journey for ships in those days.

When he arrived in Crotona he set
up a school for those interested in
mathematics. But, because such a group
would be suspected by the people who
governed the country, it became a
secret society called the Pythagoreans.
Only men were allowed to be members
of this society, and for the first
five years of membership they were not
supposed to speak, wear wool, eat
meat or beans, use iron to stir a
fire, or touch a white cockerel. Often
they did not survive the harsh diet;
but they believed that after they had
died, they would be born again,
perhaps as a dog.

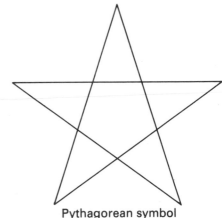

Pythagorean symbol

The Pythagoreans were responsible
for many important discoveries.
In number, Pythagoras was the first
to class numbers as odd or even. He
was interested in triangular and
square numbers. One of his most
important discoveries was the 'Theorem
of Pythagoras'. In this he said:
*In a right-angled triangle the square
on the hypotenuse is equal to the sum
of the squares on the other two sides.*

ODDS			EVENS		
1	3	5	2	4	
	7	9	8	10	6
			12		
4		9	1	3	6
16		25	10	15	21
	36	49	28	36	
SQUARES			TRIANGLES		

Exercises

1. Copy and complete the table:

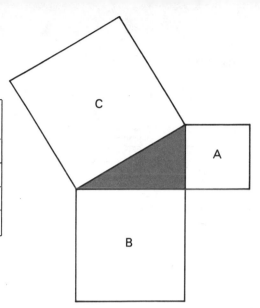

	Area of square *A*	Area of square *B*	Area of square *C*
(i)	4 cm²	9 cm²	
(ii)	9 cm²	16 cm²	
(iii)	25 cm²	49 cm²	
(iv)	36 cm²	64 cm²	

2. Copy and complete the table:

	(i)	(ii)	(iii)	(iv)
Area of square *A*	25 cm²			400 cm²
Area of square *B*		40 cm²	121 cm²	
Area of square *C*	169 cm²	100 cm²	190 cm²	625 cm²

In a right-angled triangle the side opposite the right angle is called the hypotenuse.

Exercise

3. Copy and complete the table:

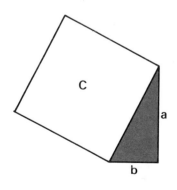

	Length of *a*	Length of *b*	Area of *C*
(i)	3 cm	5 cm	
(ii)	6 cm	8 cm	
(iii)	4 cm	6 cm	
(iv)	9 cm	10 cm	
(v)	10 m	12 m	
(vi)	8 m	13 m	
(vii)	20 m	30 m	
(viii)	1 km	2 km	
(ix)	4 km	5 km	

Squares

For discussion

    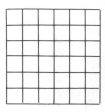

$1 \times 1 = 1$	$1^2 = 1$	$1 \rightarrow 1$
$2 \times 2 = 4$	$2^2 = 4$	$4 \rightarrow 2$
$3 \times 3 = 9$	$3^2 = 9$	$9 \rightarrow 3$
$4 \times 4 = 16$	$4^2 = 16$	$16 \rightarrow 4$
$5 \times 5 = 25$	$5^2 = 25$	$25 \rightarrow 5$
$6 \times 6 = 36$	$6^2 = 36$	$36 \rightarrow 6$

Exercises

1. Copy and complete:

   (a) $7^2 = \square$; (b) $9^2 = \square$; (c) $12^2 = \square$; (d) $15^2 = \square$; (e) $20^2 = \square$.

2. Complete (Worksheet 12), using an arrow for *is the square of*:

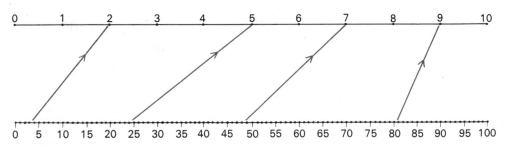

For discussion

What can you say about $(3 \cdot 5)^2$?
Is it more than 9? Is it less than 16?
Does it help to think of it as $(3\frac{1}{2})^2$?
Try to decide on a method of working it out.

Now look at the tables on the opposite page.
Can you find the value of $(3 \cdot 5)^2$ from these tables?
Is it what you thought it would be?

20   Use the Tables to find the squares of other numbers.

A table of squares

Number	Square	Number	Square	Number	Square	Number	Square
1	1	4	16	7	49	0	0
1·1	1·21	4·1	16·81	7·1	50·41	1	1
1·2	1·44	4·2	17·64	7·2	51·84	2	4
1·3	1·69	4·3	18·49	7·3	53·29	3	9
1·4	1·96	4·4	19·36	7·4	54·76	4	16
1·5	2·25	4·5	20·25	7·5	56·25	5	25
1·6	2·56	4·6	21·16	7·6	57·76	6	36
1·7	2·89	4·7	22·09	7·7	59·29	7	49
1·8	3·24	4·8	23·08	7·8	60·84	8	64
1·9	3·61	4·9	24·01	7·9	62·41	9	81
2	4	5	25	8	64	10	100
2·1	4·41	5·1	26·01	8·1	65·61	11	121
2·2	4·84	5·2	27·04	8·2	67·24	12	144
2·3	5·29	5·3	28·09	8·3	68·89	13	169
2·4	5·76	5·4	29·16	8·4	70·56	14	196
2·5	6·25	5·5	30·25	8·5	72·25	15	225
2·6	6·76	5·6	31·36	8·6	73·96	16	256
2·7	7·29	5·7	32·49	8·7	75·69	17	289
2·8	7·84	5·8	33·64	8·8	77·44	18	324
2·9	8·41	5·9	34·81	8·9	79·21	19	361
3	9	6	36	9	81	20	400
3·1	9·61	6·1	37·21	9·1	82·81		
3·2	10·24	6·2	38·44	9·2	84·64		
3·3	10·89	6·3	39·69	9·3	86·49	30	900
3·4	11·56	6·4	40·96	9·4	88·36	40	1600
3·5	12·25	6·5	42·25	9·5	90·25	50	2500
3·6	12·96	6·6	43·56	9·6	92·16	60	3600
3·7	13·69	6·7	44·89	9·7	94·09	70	4900
3·8	14·44	6·8	46·24	9·8	96·04	80	6400
3·9	15·21	6·9	47·61	9·9	98·01	90	8100
4	16	7	49	10	100	100	10000

For discussion

Look at the value of $1·6^2$. Look at the value of 16^2.
Look at $1·9^2$ and 19^2. Look at other pairs of squares like these.
What do you think is the value of 24^2? 33^2? 49^2? 63^2? 84^2?

Use the tables to find the square of:
   (a) 6·7; (b) 8·9; (c) 5·1; (d) 17; (e) 37; (f) 53; (g) 99; (h) 60; (i) 61.   **21**

Square roots

For discussion

The area of a square is 49 cm². What is the length of the side of the square?

The area of a square is 81 cm². What is the length of the side of this square?

$$\square \times \square = 64$$

Using the same number rule, what number must be put in each $\square$ to make a true statement?

The number, 8, is called the square root of 64. We write: $8 = \sqrt{64}$

Exercises

1. Copy and complete:
   (a) $\square \times \square = 81$;   (b) $\square \times \square = 121$;   (c) $\square \times \square = 36$;   (d) $\square \times \square = 169$.

2. Find: (a) $\sqrt{100}$;   (b) $\sqrt{144}$;   (c) $\sqrt{225}$;   (d) $\sqrt{196}$;   (e) $\sqrt{1}$.

3. Complete (Worksheet 12), using an arrow for *is the square root of*.

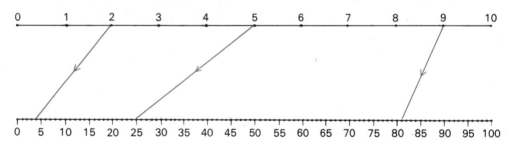

For discussion

$$\square \times \square = 20$$

What number must be put in each of the two boxes to make a true statement?
Try 4. Is it too small? Is it too big?
Try 5. Is it too small? Is it too big?
Try to decide on a way of finding the number.

Use the tables on the opposite page to find the number.
Find the square roots of other numbers.

A table of square roots (correct to two places of decimals)

Number	Square root	Number	Square root	Number	Square root	Number	Square root
1	1	26	5·10	51	7·14	76	8·72
2	1·41	27	5·20	52	7·21	77	8·78
3	1·73	28	5·29	53	7·28	78	8·83
4	2	29	5·39	54	7·35	79	8·89
5	2·24	30	5·48	55	7·42	80	8·94
6	2·45	31	5·57	56	7·48	81	9
7	2·65	32	5·66	57	7·55	82	9·06
8	2·83	33	5·75	58	7·62	83	9·11
9	3	34	5·83	59	7·68	84	9·17
10	3·16	35	5·92	60	7·75	85	9·22
11	3·32	36	6	61	7·81	86	9·27
12	3·46	37	6·08	62	7·87	87	9·33
13	3·61	38	6·16	63	7·94	88	9·38
14	3·74	39	6·25	64	8	89	9·43
15	3·87	40	6·33	65	8·06	90	9·49
16	4	41	6·40	66	8·12	91	9·54
17	4·12	42	6·48	67	8·19	92	9·59
18	4·24	43	6·56	68	8·25	93	9·64
19	4·36	44	6·63	69	8·31	94	9·70
20	4·47	45	6·71	70	8·37	95	9·75
21	4·58	46	6·78	71	8·43	96	9·80
22	4·69	47	6·86	72	8·49	97	9·85
23	4·80	48	6·93	73	8·54	98	9·90
24	4·90	49	7	74	8·60	99	9·95
25	5	50	7·07	75	8·66	100	10

Exercises

1. Copy and complete:
   (a) $\square \times \square = 15$; (b) $\square \times \square = 37$; (c) $\square \times \square = 87$; (d) $\square \times \square = 50$.

2. Find: (a) $\sqrt{43}$; (b) $\sqrt{19}$; (c) $\sqrt{8}$; (d) $\sqrt{91}$; (e) $\sqrt{40}$.

3. Find the length of the side of a square whose area is:
   (a) 41 cm²; (b) 45 cm²; (c) 85 cm²; (d) 50 cm².

4. Use the tables of squares on page 21 to find:
   (a) $\sqrt{256}$; (b) $\sqrt{324}$; (c) $\sqrt{289}$; (d) $\sqrt{900}$; (e) $\sqrt{3600}$.

For discussion

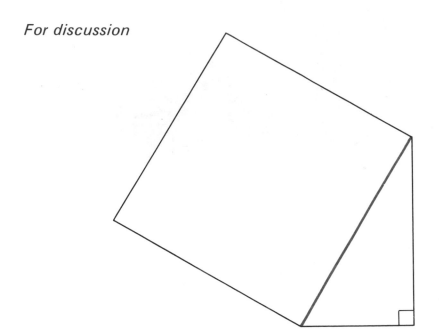

Measure the length of the shortest side of the right-angled triangle.
What would be the area of a square drawn on this side?

Measure the length of the next shortest side.
What would be the area of a square drawn on this side?

What is the area of the square drawn on the hypotenuse?

Use the square-root tables to find the length of the hypotenuse.
Check your result by measuring.

Exercise

Find the length of the hypotenuse:

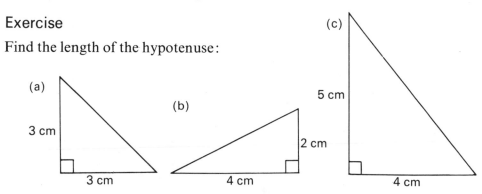

Check your results by drawing.

Exercises

1. A gate has been partly constructed and needs a diagonal strut to be fixed, as shown by the coloured dotted line. This should prevent the gate from collapsing.

   How long must the strut be?

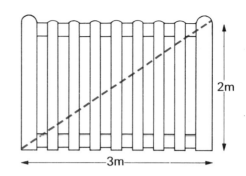

2. Three holes have to be drilled in a rectangular piece of metal.

   The diagram shows that these holes form the vertices of a right-angled triangle.
   Some distances between the centres of the holes are given.

   By an accurate drawing show the positions of the three holes.

   Measure the distance not given (the hypotenuse of the triangle).
   Check the accuracy of your drawing by calculating the length of the hypotenuse.

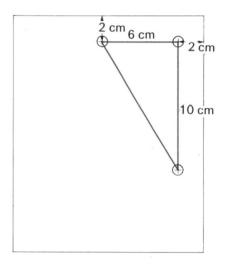

3. The drawing shows the roof timbers of a house.

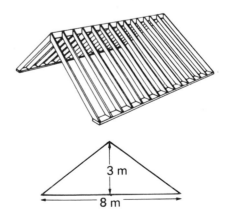

   The diagram below the drawing shows some dimensions of the roof.

   What length timbers are needed for the sloping part of the roof?

25

Exercises

1.

$$1 \qquad\qquad = \square$$
$$1+3 \qquad\quad\; = \square$$
$$1+3+5 \qquad = \square$$
$$1+3+5+7 \;\;= \square$$
$$1+3+5+7+9= \square$$

Copy and complete to make true statements.
What kind of numbers have you been adding?
What can you say about the $\square$ numbers?

Now find the sum of:
(a) the first six odd numbers;   (b) the first seven odd numbers;
(c) the first eight odd numbers;   (d) the first nine odd numbers.

Here are the results in a table:
N is used for *the number of odd numbers*
(always starting with 1).
S is used for *the sum of the odd numbers*.

Write a statement showing the relationship
between N and S.

How would you show the relationship if the
arrows were drawn in the opposite direction?

N		S
1	$\longrightarrow$	1
2	$\longrightarrow$	4
3	$\longrightarrow$	9
4	$\longrightarrow$	16
5	$\longrightarrow$	25
6	$\longrightarrow$	36
7	$\longrightarrow$	49
8	$\longrightarrow$	64
9	$\longrightarrow$	81

2. In the centre of a large sheet of
paper draw a right-angled triangle
as shown in (a). 1 decimetre (dm)$=10$ cm.
Colour the hypotenuse.
$$(\text{Hypotenuse})^2 \;=\; 1^2+1^2$$
$$=\; 2.$$
$$\text{Hypotenuse} \;=\; \sqrt{2}.$$

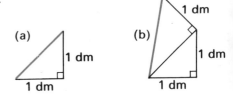

(a)   (b)

Measure the hypotenuse, to the nearest
millimetre.

On the hypotenuse draw a second
right-angled triangle to get the shape
shown in (b). What is the length of the
hypotenuse of this triangle? Measure it.
Continue in this way and so find $\sqrt{4}$, $\sqrt{5}$, etc.
Use the square-root tables to check your results.

(c)

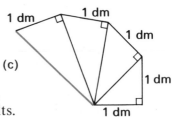

26

A CARD TRICK

You need a pack of playing cards.

Choose any card from the pack and place
it in front of you.
Now perform the following calculations.

Look at the number on the card.
(Count Ace as 1, Jack as 11,
Queen as 12 and King as 13.)

Double this number.   10

Add 1 to this result.   11

Now multiply by 5.   55

If the card is   a club: *add 6*
               a diamond: *add 7*
               a heart: *add 8*
               a spade: *add 9*   64

*Record the card you chose and
the final result of your calculation.*   5 of spades ⟶— 64

Do this with several cards.
Can you see how to tell which card was chosen by looking at the final result?
Which card was chosen if the result was 72? 133? 104?

When you have found out how to do this, ask a friend to choose a card from
the pack without letting you see it.
Then ask him or her to perform the calculations above and give you the
final result.

Using this result you should be able to tell your friends the card chosen.   **27**

SPEEDING UP CALCULATIONS

For discussion

In which of the following would it be reasonable to change the order of the two activities?
  (a) Put on your socks then put on your shoes.
  (b) Switch on the engine then press the starter.
  (c) Open the door then go into the room.
  (d) Drink your tea then eat your cake.
  (e) Pour out the tea then put in the milk.
  (f) Get into bed then go to sleep.

Make up some more examples like these and say whether you get the same result when the order is changed.

Look at this pair of statements:

$$8 + 4 = \square$$
$$4 + 8 = \square$$

What can you say about the $\square$ numbers?
Is this true for any pair of numbers?

Replace the $+$ sign by a $-$ sign.
What can you say now?

Replace the $+$ sign by a $\times$ sign.
What can you say in this case?

Replace the $+$ sign by a $\div$ sign.
What are the $\square$ numbers now?

Start with another pair of numbers and repeat the above activity.
Try some more.

Can you make up a rule about what happens when you change the order of the two numbers?

What happens when one of the two numbers is 1?

28   What happens when one of the two numbers is 0?

Exercises

1. Which of the following statements are true?
   - (a) $5 \times 7 = 7 \times 5$
   - (b) $18 + 17 = 17 + 18$
   - (c) $55 - 29 = 29 - 55$
   - (d) $6 \div 3 = 3 \div 6$
   - (e) $99 \times 45 = 45 \times 99$
   - (f) $84 \div 21 = 21 \div 84$
   - (g) $9 - 4 = 4 - 9$
   - (h) $87 + 78 = 78 + 87$
   - (i) $47 - 39 = 39 - 47$

2. Copy and complete the statement.
   - (a) $13 \times 1 = \square$
   - (b) $141 + 0 = \square$
   - (c) $1 \times 299 = \square$
   - (d) $0 \times 7 = \square$
   - (e) $954 \times 0 = \square$
   - (f) $0 \div 300 = \square$
   - (g) $0 \div 4 = \square$
   - (h) $500 \times 1 = \square$
   - (i) $0 \times 999 = \square$

3. Look at the table.
   Can you see how to use it?

   Can you see, from the work you have been doing, a quick way of filling in the gaps?

   Copy and complete the table.

×	10	11	12	13	14	15	16	17	18	19	20
10	100										
11	110	121									
12	120	132	144								
13	130	143	156	169							
14	140	154	168	182	196						
15	150	165	180	195	210	225					
16	160	176	192	208	224	240	256				
17	170	187	204	221	238	255	272	289			
18	180	198	216	234	252	270	288	306	324		
19	190	209	228	247	266	285	304	323	342	361	
20	200	220	240	260	280	300	320	340	360	380	400

4. Here are some tables in which a number base other than ten is used.

base five

+	0	1	2	3	4
0	0		2	3	
1	1	2	3		10
2			4		
3		4	10	11	
4	4			11	12	13

base eight

×	0	1	2	3	4	5	6	7
0	0							
1		1						
2			4	6		12	14	
3				11	14		22	25
4			10		20		30	
5				17	24	31	36	
6							44	52
7			16		34	43		61

base three

×	0	1	2
0			
1			
2			11

Copy and complete the tables.

For discussion

Look at this pair of statements.

$$12+(6+2) = \square$$
$$(12+6)+2 = \square$$

What can you say about the $\square$ numbers?
Is this true for any three numbers?

Replace each of the four addition signs by a subtraction sign.
(Remember to work the part in the bracket first.)
What can you say now?

Go on to replace each of the addition signs by:
(a) a multiplication sign; (b) a division sign.

Repeat all these changes for other sets of three numbers (e.g. 24, 8, 2).

Now try replacing the *first* addition sign in each statement by another sign.
(Use the same sign in each case.)

Go on to see what happens when the *second* (but not the first) addition sign in each statement is replaced by another sign.

Can you now make up a rule which tells you what signs you can use so that the position of the brackets does not affect the result?

Exercises

1. Which of the following statements are true?
   (a) $4+(3+9)=(4+3)+9$ (b) $12-(6-2)=(12-6)-2$
   (c) $8 \times (3 \times 5)=(8 \times 3) \times 5$ (d) $(36 \div 6) \div 3 = 36 \div (6 \div 3)$
   (e) $80-(40-19)=(80-40)-19$ (f) $79+(64+27)=(79+64)+27$
   (g) $(17 \times 19) \times 21 = 17 \times (19 \times 21)$ (h) $144 \div (24 \div 3)=(144 \div 24) \div 3$

2. Copy and complete the statement, putting in brackets to show which pair of numbers you dealt with first.
   (a) $8+2+19=\square$ (b) $67+1+99=\square$ (c) $17+3+60=\square$
   (d) $2 \times 5 \times 16=\square$ (e) $9 \times 2 \times 4 =\square$ (f) $5 \times 4 \times 15=\square$

30   3. Find the value of: (a) $17 \times 0 \times 6$; (b) $166 \times 199 \times 0$; (c) $1 \times 1 \times 1 \times 1$.

For discussion

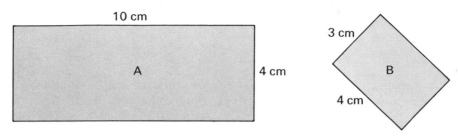

Find the total area of the two rectangles, *A* and *B*, in as many ways as you can.

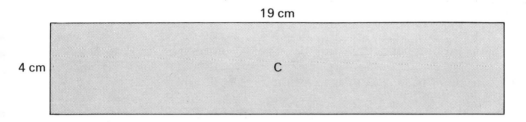

We could find the area of rectangle *C* by finding the value of 4×19.
An easier way might be to divide the rectangle into two smaller rectangles and add together the areas of the two parts.
How would you divide it?

Is it true that $4 \times 19 = (4 \times 10) + (4 \times 9)$?

Is it true that $4 \times 19 = (4 \times 20) - (4 \times 1)$?

Exercises

1. Find the value of:
   (a) 4×18 (b) 7×16 (c) 9×13 (d) 8×17
   (e) 5×24 (f) 6×26 (g) 4×29 (h) 9×32

2. Find the value of:
   (a) 10×18 (b) 20×18 (c) 5×18 (d) 25×18
   (e) 10×16 (f) 30×16 (g) 7×16 (h) 37×16
   (i) 10×23 (j) 40×23 (k) 8×23 (l) 48×23

3. Find the value of:
   (a) 19×15 (b) 17×16 (c) 14×28 (d) 13×45
   (e) 28×31 (f) 34×34 (g) 42×53 (h) 63×76

Most of us welcome ways of doing calculations quickly and with as little effort as possible. One of these ways—used by engineers and scientists—is described in the next few pages.

Look at the opposite page. Look at the three numbered lines **A**, **B** and **C**. (*Note:* numbered lines like these are often called scales.)

What do you notice about the numbers on **A**, **B** and **C**?

Look at the coloured line.
It represents the edge of a ruler placed so that it passes through the point 8 on the **A** scale and the point 14 on the **B** scale.

What is the number of the point that it passes through on the **C** scale?

Choose other pairs of numbers, one on the **A** scale and the other on the **B** scale.
For each pair use your ruler to find the number on the **C** scale. Record your results on a table, as shown.

A	B	C
8	14	22
7	18	

Can you say what these scales are being used to do?

Can you see how to use the scales for subtraction?

Exercise

1. Use the scales to find the value of:
    (a) 23 + 8   (b) 17 + 19   (c) 33 − 17   (d) 27 − 9
    (e) 15 + 19   (f) 21 − 6   (g) 19 + 19   (h) 36 − 18

For discussion

Can you see how to find the value of 12·4 + 6·8 using the scales?
Can you see how to find the value of 26·2 − 7·4 using the scales?

Exercise

2. Use the scales to find the value of:
    (a) 14·6 + 17·4   (b) 8·9 + 7·5   (c) 17·5 − 9·7   (d) 15 − 8·8
    (e) 21·5 − 9·7   (f) 19·8 + 9·8   (g) 20 − 15·5   (h) 17 + 9·7

A set of scales like these is called a nomogram.

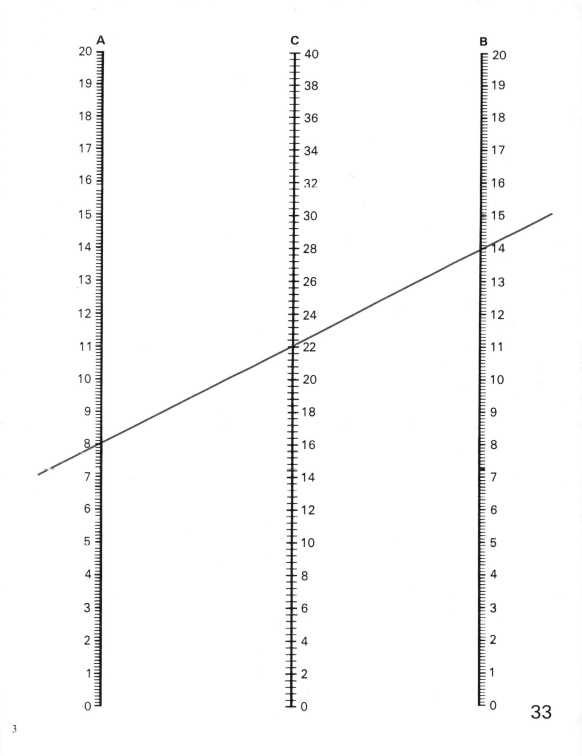

33

3

For discussion

In the nomogram on the previous page the **C** scale was midway between the **A** scale and the **B** scale.
Also there were twice as many numbers marked on the **C** scale as on each of the other two scales.

Now look at the nomogram on the opposite page.
The **C** scale is not now midway between the other two scales.
The distance between the **C** and **B** scales is twice the distance between the **C** and **A** scales.

Look at the numbers on the three scales. Look at the small divisions. What does each division represent on **A**? on **B**? on **C**?

Look at the coloured line drawn across the scales.
Which points does it pass through?

A	B	C
10	14	34
12	8	

Place the edge of a ruler so that it passes through the point 12 on the **A** scale and the point 8 on the **B** scale. Which point does it pass through on the **C** scale?

Repeat for many other pairs of numbers.

Record the results in a table as shown.

What calculation is being done in each case?

If a is the number on the **A** scale, b the number on the **B** scale and c the number on the **C** scale, can you write down a statement to show the relationship between a, b and c?

Exercises

1. Use the nomogram to find the value of:
   - (a) $5+(2\times 9)$
   - (b) $9+(2\times 16)$
   - (c) $(2\times 8)+13$
   - (d) $12+(2\times 9{\cdot}5)$
   - (e) $(2\times 8{\cdot}5)+16{\cdot}5$
   - (f) $7\frac{1}{2}+(2\times 14\frac{1}{2})$
   - (g) 3×9
   - (h) $3\times 17{\cdot}5$

2. a, b and c are numbers such that $c=(2\times a)+b$.
   Use the nomogram to find a when $b=9$ and $c=35$.
   Also find b when $a=17$ and $c=43$.

34 3. Design, and then draw, a nomogram for $c=(3\times a)+b$.

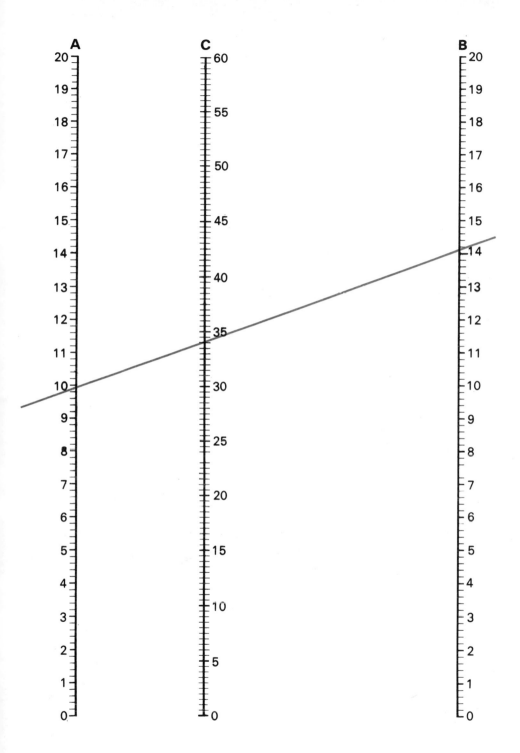

35

For discussion

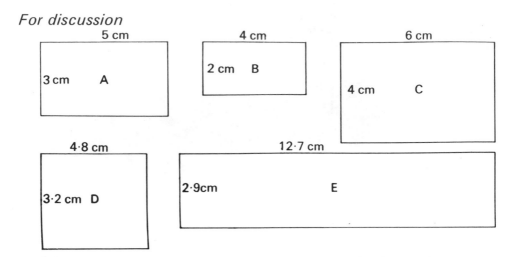

How would you find the perimeter of each of the rectangles drawn above?

If you had a suitable nomogram you could read off the answers.
Can you suggest a way of designing the nomogram?

The scales for the length and width are drawn on the opposite page.
The line for the perimeter scale is drawn mid-way between the other two but it is not numbered.

Do you agree that the perimeter of the first rectangle shown above is 16 cm?
Place a straight edge across the 5 mark on the length scale and the 3 mark on the width scale (Worksheet 13).
Mark the point where it crosses the perimeter line.
Write 16 at the side of the point.

Use another length and width to mark and number a second point on the perimeter scale.
Continue in this way until you have a reasonable number of points on the scale.
Can you suggest a quicker method of numbering the scale?

Exercises

1. Use your nomogram to find the perimeter of each of the rectangles above.

2. Use your nomogram to complete this table:

Length	14 cm	11·6 cm	8 cm	9 m	8 cm		15 cm
Width	9 cm	9·8 cm	$5\frac{1}{2}$ cm	14 m		14 m	15 cm
Perimeter					30 cm	58 m	

A nomogram for the length, width and perimeter of a rectangle

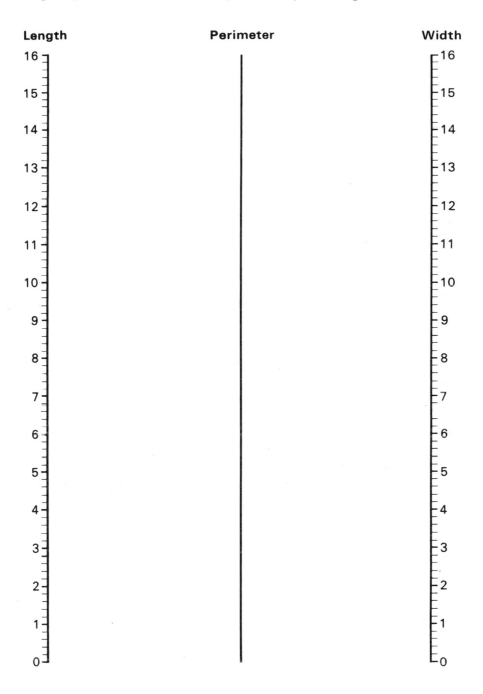

Length

Perimeter

Width

For discussion

Look at the nomogram on the opposite page.
What do you think it will help you to do?

Look at the way in which the *Length* scale
is marked.
How many divisions are there between 1 and 2?
How many are there between other whole
numbers?

Point to the place on the scale for:
3·5, 4·7, 5·4, 8·6, 9·8, 1·5, 5·5, 6·1, 7·3.

What do you notice about the *Width* scale?

Now look at the way in which the *Area*
scale is marked.
Look at the small divisions *very* carefully.
Point to the place on the scale for:
12, 26, 44, 55, 85, 1·8, 3·2, 4·8, 5·5, 9·5.

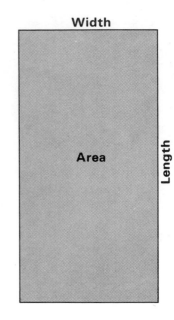

Two copies of the *Area* scale are drawn on Worksheet 14.
On the first of these some points are indicated by arrows.
Give the number for each of these points as accurately as you can.
On the other scale mark the point for: 15, 27, 54, 81, 9·6, 2·9, 3·7, 5.

Note: Scales marked like those on this nomogram are called logarithmic
scales. They are like the scales on your circular slide rule.

Exercises

1. Use the nomogram to complete this table:

Length	8 cm	6·4 cm	3·9 cm	7 cm		3·95 cm
Width	5 cm	4·5 cm	7·9 cm		5·2 cm	
Area				56 cm²	48·5 cm²	17 cm²

2. Can you see how to use the nomogram to find squares and square roots of
   numbers?

3. A farmer has 24 metres of fencing with which to make a rectangular pen.
   Use your Perimeter nomogram and the Area nomogram to:
   (a) Write down some possible lengths and widths of the pen;
   (b) Find the dimensions of the pen with the largest area.

A nomogram for the length, width and area of a rectangle

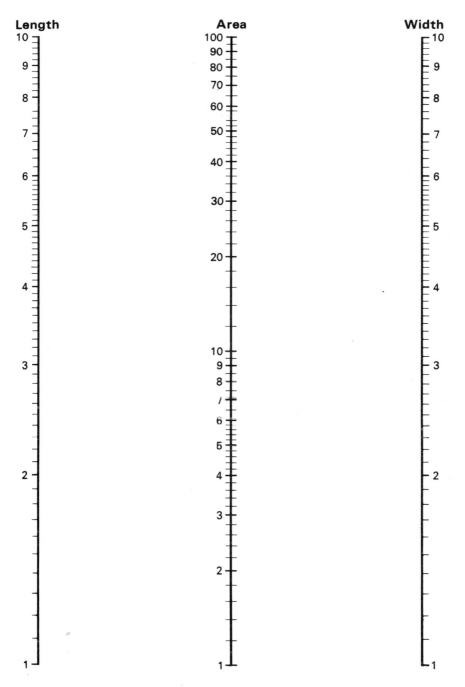

39

NUMBER PATTERNS

For the work which follows it would be advisable to work in pairs, each pair attempting one or two of the activities.

1. *Dots and lines*

Place three dots on your paper (not in a straight line).
How many straight lines can be drawn having a dot at each end?
Now try this with four dots (making sure that no three dots are in a straight line). How many straight lines can be drawn now?
Repeat this for 2, 5, 6, 7 and 8 dots and record the results on a table.

2. *Binary numbers*

base ten	base two
0	0
1	1
2	10
3	11
4	100
5	101

Write all the numbers from 0 to 15 in the binary system.
Now make a table of the binary numbers collecting together numbers which have the same number of 1s, e.g.:

No 1s	One 1	Two 1s	Three 1s	Four 1s
0	1 10 100	11 101		

Count and record the number of binary numbers in each column.
Repeat this for binary numbers from: (a) 0 to 7; (b) 0 to 31.

40

3. *Powers of eleven*

$$11^1 = 11$$
$$11^2 = 121$$
$$11^3 =$$
$$11^4 =$$
$$11^5 =$$

Copy and complete this table.

4. *Choices*

The school tennis team is one player short. The vacant place can be filled
by one of three girls, Andrea (A), Beryl (B) and Carol (C).
How many choices are there?
If the team is two players short and the vacant places can be filled by any
two of A, B and C, how many choices are there?
How many choices are there if three places have to be filled?
Record your results on a table as shown.

Number of places to be filled	1	2	3
Number of choices			

Now try this again when the vacant places can be filled by four girls, A, B, C
and D. Record your results as shown.

Number of places to be filled	1	2	3	4
Number of choices				

41

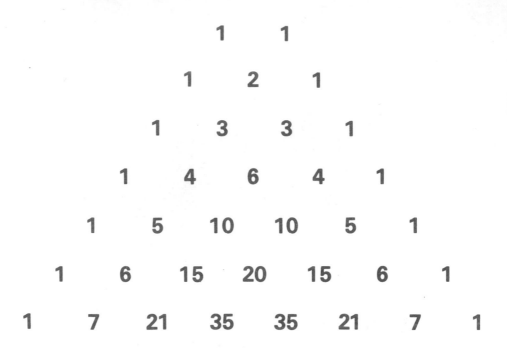

Do you recognize these numbers? You met them in your work for page 6, where this array of numbers was called Pascal's triangle.
How would you find the numbers of the next row?
Copy the triangle of numbers and add a further two rows.

In the activities you have been doing from the previous two pages, you have recorded some numbers. These numbers all have a connection with Pascal's triangle.
Can you find your results in the triangle?

Use Pascal's triangle to answer the following questions.

(a) *Dots and lines:* How many straight lines could be drawn using 9 dots?

(b) *Binary numbers:* If all the numbers from 0 to 63 were written in the binary system, how many of these numbers would contain two 1's?

(c) *Powers of eleven:* What is the value of 11^6?

(d) *Choices:* If five girls are available to fill two places in a tennis team, how many choices are there?

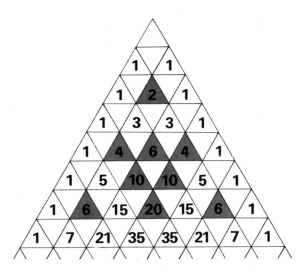

On the Pascal's triangle above, all the *even* numbers have been coloured.
In the same way colour all the even numbers on Worksheet 15.
Comment on the pattern you get.

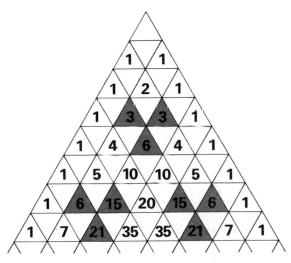

On this Pascal's triangle all numbers which are a *multiple of 3* have been
coloured.
In the same way colour all the *multiples of 3* on Worksheet 16.
Comment on the pattern you get.

Using Worksheet 17, colour some other kind of number and comment on the
pattern produced.

43

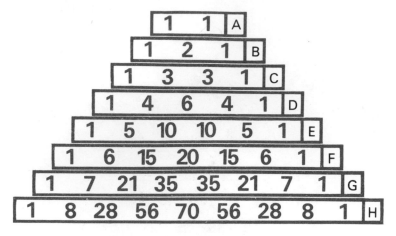

The diagram shows some rows of Pascal's triangle written on strips.
The strips are labelled *A, B, C, D, E, F, G* and *H*.
Using Worksheet 18, stick the strips on card and then cut them out.

Add the numbers on strip *A*. What is the total?
Add the numbers on strip *B*. What is the total?
Do this for each of the strips, recording your results.
What do you notice about these numbers?
Can you give the result of adding the numbers on the next strip?
And the next?
Write each of the totals as a power of 2. What do you notice?

Now rearrange strips *A, B, C* and *D* so that the numbers are in columns, like this:

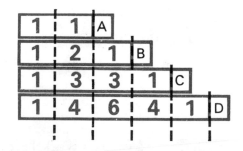

Add the numbers in each of the columns. What do you notice?

44 Compare the totals with the numbers on strip *E*.

If the strips are placed like this:

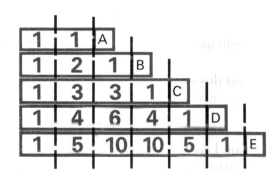

You see that the numbers on strip E give the results of adding the columns (except for the first column).

Now rearrange strips A, B, C, D and E like this:

Add the numbers in each of the columns.
Does strip F give the results?
Repeat using more strips and see if the next strip gives the results.

Exercises

Use Pascal's triangle on Worksheet 15 to answer the following questions.
1. What is the value of $1+2+3+4+5+6+7+8+9$?
2. What is the value of $1+2+3+4+5+- - - - - - +11+12+13$?
3. Write the following numbers and continue the sequence until you have ten numbers: 1, 3, 6, 10, – – – – – –.
4. What is the result of adding the ten numbers from Exercise 3?

45

Now arrange all your strips in this way:

1	1	A							
	1	2	1	B					
		1	3	3	1	C			
			1	4	6	4	1	D	
				1	5	10	10	5	1	E
					1	6	15	20	15	6	1	F
						1	7	21	35	35	21	7
							1	8	28	56	70	56

| 1 | 2 | 3 | | | | | | | |

Add the numbers in each of the first eight columns and record the results.
(You must not go beyond the eighth column unless you put further strips in the pattern.)

You should now have eight numbers in a sequence which begins: 1, 2, 3, 5, ...

What do you notice about this sequence of numbers?
Can you continue the sequence?

An Italian mathematician, Leonardo de Pisa (nicknamed Fibonacci), who lived from about A.D. 1170 to A.D. 1250 became very interested in this sequence of numbers. He had, however, another '1' at the beginning of his sequence. So his sequence was 1, 1, 2, 3, 5, 8, ...
This sequence of numbers is known as the Fibonacci sequence.
In 1963 a group of people became interested in this sequence of numbers and formed a society called the Fibonacci Association. Within two years the Association published some 600 pages of the results of their investigations into the sequence.

On the next two pages some of the interesting and rather strange properties of these numbers are discussed. You might, however, like to investigate them yourself before going on further.

The Fibonacci numbers

1, 1, 2, 3, 5, 8, 13, 21, 34, 55, 89, 144, – – – – –

For discussion

(a)

| 2, 3, 5, 8 |

Multiply the two *outside* numbers. ($2 \times 8 = 16$)
Multiply the two *inside* numbers. ($3 \times 5 = 15$)
The difference between these results is 1.
Try this with other sets of four numbers which follow each other in the
sequence. Does it always work?

(b)

| 2, 3, 5 |

Multiply together the two outside numbers   ($2 \times 5 = 10$).
Square the middle number.   ($3^2 = 9$).
The difference between these results is 1.
Try this with other sets of three numbers which follow each other in the
sequence. Does it always work?

(c)

| 1, 1, 2, 3, 5, 8 |

Square each of the first *five* numbers and add the results.
$$1^2 + 1^2 + 2^2 + 3^2 + 5^2 = 1 + 1 + 4 + 9 + 25$$
$$= 40$$
Multiply the *last two* numbers ($5 \times 8 = 40$).
The results are the same.
Now use the first 7 numbers. Square and add the first 6. Multiply the sixth
and seventh. What do you notice? Go on to use the first 8, 9, ...

(d) Use Worksheets 19 and 20.
Find the regular pentagon whose side is 3 cm.
Measure and record (in cm) the length of
a diagonal.

Repeat for a regular pentagon of side:
(i) 5 cm;   (ii) 8 cm;
What do you notice?
What do you think is the approximate
length of the diagonal of a regular pentagon
with sides (i) 13 cm? (ii) 21 cm?

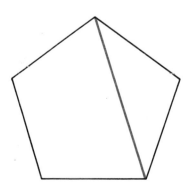

47

(e)

The scales in this pine cone form spirals: some in a clockwise direction and some in an anti-clockwise direction.

Count the number of spirals in each direction.

The spirals found on daisy heads are often 5 one way and 8 the other.
The bumps on pineapples often form spirals, 8 one way and 13 the other.

(f) Start with a rectangular piece of paper, measuring 34 cm by 21 cm. Record the length and width.
Remove from one end a square, as shown. Measure and record the length of the remaining piece.
In the same way remove a square from this piece. Measure the new remaining piece and record.
Go on doing this. (You should finish with a one-centimetre square.)

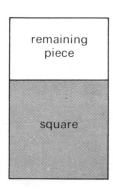

The Parthenon at Athens was built by the Greeks in the fifth century B.C.
The ruins still remain, as shown in the photograph at the bottom.

The drawing shows the front of the completed building, surrounded by a
coloured rectangle. Measure the sides of this rectangle in centimetres?
Can you see a relation between the measurements and the numbers in the
Fibonacci sequence? (It will help to double the measurements.)

4

Digit-Ad

For discussion

Think of a number, say 126.
Add the digits of the number. $(1+2+6=9)$
Call the total the digit-sum of the number. (The digit-sum of 126 is 9.)

What is the digit-sum of: (a) 213? (b) 52? (c) 17? (d) 8?

Sometimes the total is more than 9.
For example the total of the digits of 157 is 13. $(1+5+7=13)$
In cases like this the digits of the total are themselves added. $(1+3=4)$
This second total is now the digit-sum.
So the digit-sum of 157 is 4.

What is the digit sum of: (a) 56? (b) 185? (c) 78? (d) 576? (e) 64?

Look at the two columns of numbers.

3	3
6	6
9	9
12	3
15	6
18	9
21	3
24	6
27	9
30	3
33	6
36	9
39	3
42	6
45	9
48	3
51	6
54	9
57	3
60	6

The first column gives some multiples of 3.
The second column gives the digit-sums of the multiples.

What do you notice about the numbers in the second column?

The pattern of the digit-sums gives a way of telling whether or not a number is a multiple of 3.

For instance: is 152 a multiple of 3?
   Find the digit-sum of 152. $(1+5+2=8)$
   The result is not 3, 6 or 9 so 152 is
   not a multiple of 3.

Exercise

Find which of these numbers is a multiple of 3:

(a)	78	(b)	144	(c)	72	(d)	451
(e)	576	(f)	1001	(g)	1234	(h)	8888
(i)	111	(j)	1111	(k)	11111	(l)	111111

For discussion

The pattern of the digit-sums of multiples of 3 can be shown on a circle.
Nine equally spaced points are marked on the circle and numbered 1 to 9.
Show the pattern, 3, 6, 9, 3, 6, 9, . . . ,
by joining 3 → 6, 6 → 9, 9 → 3.

3	3
6	6
9	9
12	3
15	6
18	9
21	3
24	6
27	9
30	3

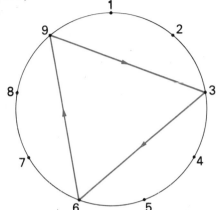

The multiples of 7 and their digit-sums are shown below.
The pattern of the digit-sums on a circle has been started.
What do you think the
completed pattern will be ?

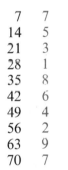

7	7
14	5
21	3
28	1
35	8
42	6
49	4
56	2
63	9
70	7

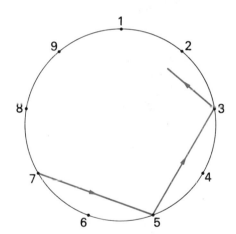

Copy and complete the pattern on the circle (Worksheet 21).

Exercise

Use the marked circles on Worksheets 21 and 22 to investigate the pattern
of the digit-sums for multiples of:

(a) 2	(b) 4	(c) 5	(d) 6
(e) 8	(f) 9	(g) 11	(h) 12

DISTANCE, TIME, SPEED

For discussion

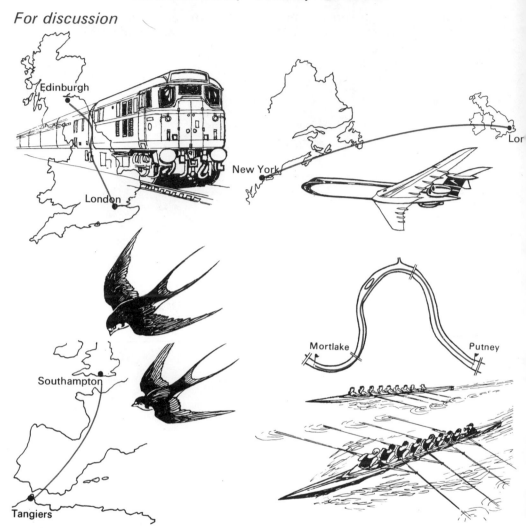

Look at each of the drawings in turn.

They all show some way of travelling from one place to another.

Find out how far it is between the two places mentioned on each drawing.

Find out how long it will take to travel this distance for each 'traveller' mentioned.

Use other examples if it is more convenient to do so.

What can you say about the speed of each traveller?

For discussion

The drawing shows part of town with a route marked from a school to the swimming pool.
The length of the route is $\frac{1}{2}$ kilometre.

Find a landmark in your own district which is $\frac{1}{2}$ kilometre from some part of your school.

Walk to the landmark and back to school.
How long did it take you?

Were you able to go at the same speed for the whole journey?
Were you held up at traffic lights? Were some roads more crowded than others? Did it make a difference whether you were going uphill or down?

If you kept on walking in this way for an hour about how many kilometres would you go?
What do you understand by *average speed*?

Average speed

For discussion

A car goes at an average speed of 50 km/h.
How far will it go in: (a) 2 hours?   (b) 3 hours?   (c) ½ hour?
(d) 1½ hours?   (e) 2½ hours?   (f) 24 minutes?

Can you see how to use the nomogram on the opposite page to find some of the answers?

A car travels 80 kilometres in 1½ hours.
Use the nomogram to find the average speed.

A man walks 20 kilometres at an average speed of 4½ km/h.
Use the nomogram to find the time he takes.

Exercises

1. Use the nomogram to find, as accurately as you can, the average speed of:
   (a) a cyclist travelling 70 kilometres in 3 hours;
   (b) a cyclist travelling 90 kilometres in 2½ hours;
   (c) a cyclist travelling 26 kilometres in 1½ hours;
   (d) George Bouton's steam quadrille which, in 1887, travelled 32 kilometres in approximately 1¼ hours.

2. Use the nomogram to find, as accurately as you can, the distance travelled when:
   (a) a car travels for 2½ hours at an average speed of 28 km/h;
   (b) a train travels for 1½ hours at an average speed of 65 km/h;
   (c) a man walks for 2¼ hours at an average speed of 4·6 km/h;
   (d) a cyclist averages 19 km/h for 2¾ hours.

3. Use the nomogram to find, as accurately as you can, the time taken when:
   (a) a bus goes 87 kilometres at an average speed of 39 km/h;
   (b) a train goes 96 kilometres at an average speed of 59 km/h
   (c) a motor-cyclist goes 80 kilometres at an average speed of 100 km/h;
   (d) a bird flies 39 kilometres at an average speed of 60 km/h.

4. See if you can use the nomogram to find:
   (a) the average speed of a car which goes 400 kilometres in 4½ hours;
   (b) the time taken by a car which goes 92 kilometres at a speed of 55 km/h;
   (c) the average speed of an aeroplane which travels 2400 kilometres in 3½ hours.

A nomogram for distance, time and average speed

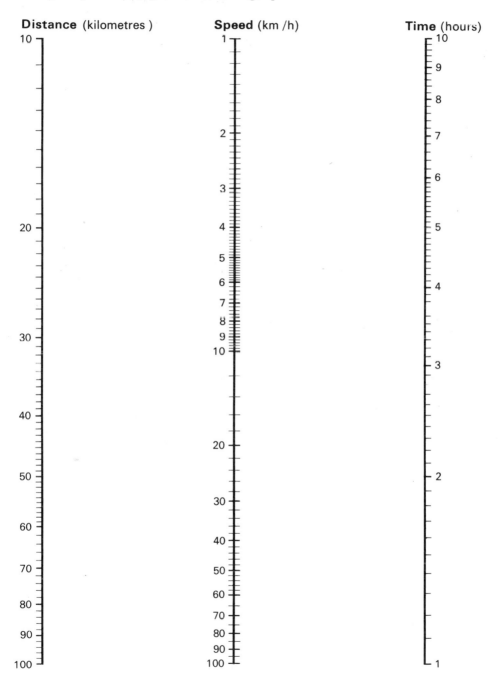

Distance (kilometres)

Speed (km /h)

Time (hours)

55

A graph of a train journey

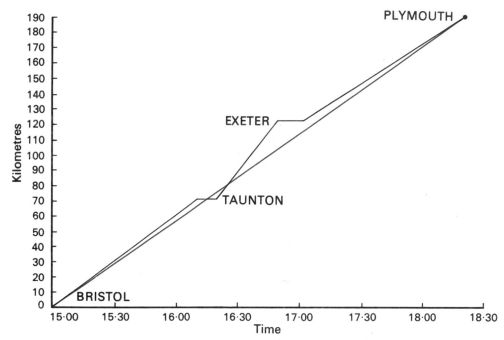

At each of the towns the graph has a horizontal portion.
What does this tell you?

How do the stops effect the average speed over the whole journey?

What does the coloured line show?

Exercises   You need an up-to-date timetable and an old train timetable for the same region.

1. Copy a small part of a train timetable.
   Graph the part you have copied.
   Between which stations is the speed greatest?
   Can you find a reason for this.
   Put a coloured line on your graph to indicate average speed.
   What is the average speed over the whole journey?

2. Try to obtain a train timetable for several years ago. Repeat Exercise 1.
   What do you notice?
   Can you explain any differences?

Units of speed

Speed is described in many ways. Some of these are:

> *metres per second*   m/s
> *kilometres per hour*   km/h
> *(for air and sea travel)* knots

Say which of these would be a useful way of describing the speed of:

a cricket ball

a racing car

a river

a chip

Exercises (Worksheets 23, 24)

1. Find out all you can about knots.
   Why is a knot used as a unit of speed for air and sea travel?

2. Draw a conversion graph for km/h and knots (20 km/h $\simeq$ 11 knots).
   Find the usual speeds for some boats and ships.
   What would these speeds be in km/h?
   Find some of the record speeds, over the last 50 years, for ships crossing
   the Atlantic Ocean.

3. Draw a conversion graph for km/h and m/s (18 km/h = 5 m/s).
   Find the speeds of some of the following in m/s:
   clockwork trains, model electric trains, model racing cars, friction toys.
   What are their speeds in km/h?

Speeds of human beings

For discussion

In the 1968 Olympic Games in Mexico the 1500 metres race was won by Kipchoge Keino in a time of 3 minutes 34·9 seconds.

His average speed was 25·1 km/h (1000 m = 1 km).

Exercises You need records of previous Olympic Games.

1. Collect information about previous Olympic Games results for the 1500 metres. Draw a graph to show how the average speed has changed. How do these speeds compare with your school records?

2. Collect information about distance and time for different track events, the marathon, swimming events, cycle races, etc. Find the average speed for each.

3. How fast can you run: (a) 100 metres?
                            (b) 1 kilometre?

Collect school results for running, swimming, cycling, etc. and compare the average speeds.

Speeds of animals

Many animals and birds are capable of great speeds.
This is often necessary to catch other animals for food or to escape from being caught.
Here are some speeds of animals and birds.

Over very short distances the fastest of all land animals is the cheetah. Speeds of up to 135 km/h have been recorded.

Probably the fastest moving creature is the spine-tailed swift which is said to have reached a speed of 320 km/h over a 3-kilometre distance in India. Racing pigeons have been known to fly an an average speed of 150 km/h over an 130-kilometre course.

A bee, which is said to have a maximum speed of 22 km/h, would use only one litre of nectar in cruising 1 500 000 km at 11 km/h!

Exercises You need sports results from newspapers and magazines; a stopwatch.

1. Collect information from newspapers and magazines about times taken, over different distances, for horses and dogs.
   Find approximate average speeds for these. (Use the nomogram on page 55.)

2. Try to obtain information about distances and time taken for migrating birds.
   Find the approximate average speeds.

3. Carry out some experiments yourself to find the average speeds of animals, insects and birds around you.

You need motor magazines and motor car handbooks.

1.

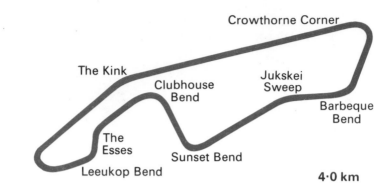

The South African Grand Prix is run over this circuit.
It is a race of 80 laps.
What is the total distance in kilometres?

In 1967 the race was won by P. Rodriguez driving a Cooper Maserati in a
time of almost 2 hours 6 minutes.
What was his approximate average speed in kilometres per hour?

The fastest lap time was set up by Jack Brabham in a Repco Brabham
with a time of 1 minute 28 seconds.
What was his average speed over this lap?

How does the average speed of this race compare with others in the Grand
Prix Competition?

2. Collect cuttings of motor-car and motor-cycle races from newspapers and
magazines.
Find out anything you wish about average speeds over complete races
or laps of any vehicle that interests you.
Collect graphs of car and motor-cycle tests and comment on them.

3. Handbooks are provided with new cars and give a lot of information about
their performance. Collect some of these books for British and foreign cars
and compare speeds in different gears for cars of similar engine size.

Newspapers and motor magazines often publish reports of trials carried
out on new cars. Compare the results of these reports with those of the
handbook.

Special units of speed

Use reference books from the library to find out all you can about the following units of speed.

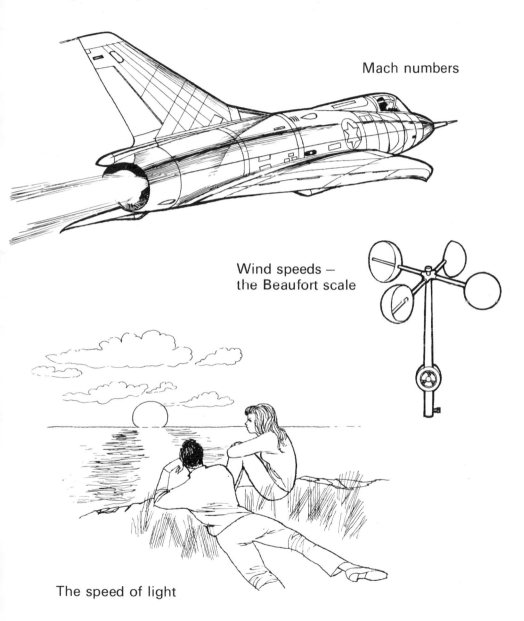

Mach numbers

Wind speeds — the Beaufort scale

The speed of light

NETWORKS

For discussion

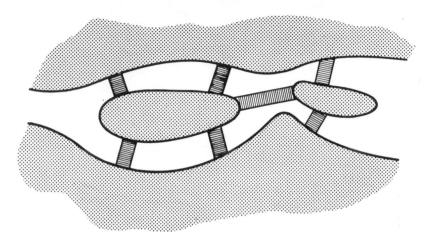

In the 18th century the people of Koenigsberg (then in Germany) had a very interesting problem.

The river Pregel flowed through the town and in it there were two islands as shown in the drawing above.

These islands and the mainland were connected by seven bridges, as shown. The problem was: is it possible to take a walk so as to cross each bridge once and once only?

The starting point can be on either of the islands or on either of the banks. The finishing point does not have to be the same as the starting point.

Try this problem yourself, using the map on Worksheet 26.

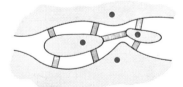  

Using the other map on Worksheet 26 mark a point on each piece of land. Now draw lines connecting these points so that you have a line over each bridge, as shown.

The problem of the Koenigsberg bridges is the same as trying to draw this network without taking your pencil off the paper and without going over any line twice. Try it!

A mathematician named Leonard Euler became interested in the Koenigsberg bridges problem. He used the idea of networks to see whether the walk could be made.

Keeping the rules:
  (a) *your pencil must not be taken off the paper*
  (b) *no line must be drawn twice*
he found a way of deciding whether a network could be drawn.

To do this he had to count the number of lines going to each point (called a junction). For each junction he then had to say whether the number of lines was odd or even.

On this network an *E* is written against a junction with an even number of lines going to it, and an *O* is written against a junction with an odd number of lines going to it.

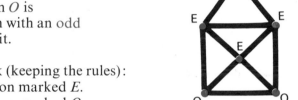

Try drawing this network (keeping the rules):
  (a) starting at a junction marked *E*.
  (b) starting at a junction marked *O*.

Exercise (Worksheet 27)

Mark each junction with an *E* or an *O* and then try to draw the network (keeping the rules, of course).

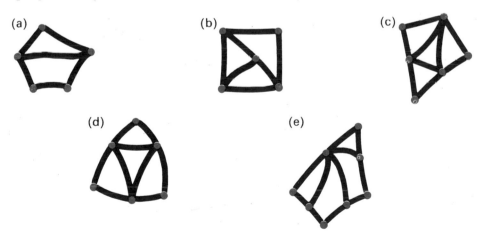

(a)

(b)

(c)

(d)

(e)

Can you now decide when it is possible to draw a network?

For discussion

This is what Euler discovered:
  A network can only be drawn (keeping the rules) if
  either (a) *it has no odd junctions*
  or   (b) *it has two odd junctions.* (In this case it can be drawn only by
            starting at an odd junction.)

Do you agree?

Using Euler's statement decide whether the Koenigsberg bridges problem can
be solved.
Is it possible to make the walk if another bridge is built? If so where would you
build it?

Exercise

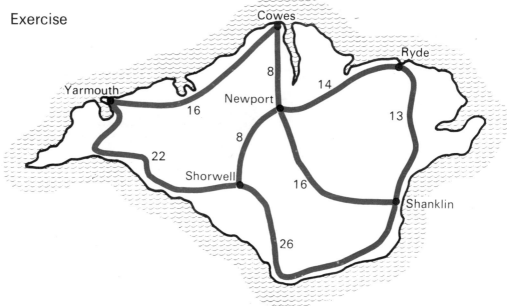

The map shows some of the roads on the Isle of Wight.
A man wishes to inspect all these roads, starting and finishing at Newport.
Is it possible to do this without going over any road twice? (Worksheet 28).

Is it possible to do it without going over any road twice, by starting at Shanklin?
Is it possible to start and finish at Shanklin?

The distances, in km, between the towns are shown on the map.
64 Work out the shortest route for the man starting and finishing at Newport.

Describing a network

For discussion

Draw a network with five junctions.
Describe this network to a friend, imagining that you are speaking over a telephone.
Ask your friend to draw this network as you describe it.
You may be surprised at the result.

Here is a way of describing a network, with four junctions, using a table.
Can you see how it works?

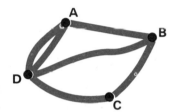

	A	B	C	D
A	0	1	0	2
B	1	0	1	1
C	0	1	0	1
D	2	1	1	0

A table which shows information in this way is called a matrix.

This matrix shows the number of lines connecting junctions.

Draw another network, with five junctions.
Label the junctions **A, B, C, D** and **E.**
Make a matrix to show the number of lines connecting junctions.
Give the matrix to a friend and ask him or her to draw the network.
Compare the result with your network.

Exercise

Draw the network described by the matrix:

(a)

	A	B	C	D
A	0	1	1	1
B	1	0	2	0
C	1	2	0	2
D	1	0	2	0

(b)

	A	B	C	D	E
A	0	1	1	1	1
B	1	0	1	0	0
C	1	1	0	1	0
D	1	0	1	0	1
E	1	0	0	1	0

(c)

	A	B	C	D
A	0	1	1	1
B	1	1	1	0
C	1	1	1	1
D	1	0	1	1

Can you tell from a matrix the number of lines going to each junction?
Can you tell from a matrix whether or not the network can be drawn, keeping to the usual rules?

5

For discussion

Here is a network on which
the spaces enclosed by the
lines have been coloured.

How many spaces are there in this network?
How many junctions are there? How many lines?

Here are some more networks with the spaces coloured.

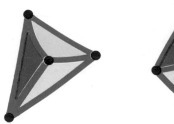  

Count the number of spaces, junctions and lines in each of these.

Leonard Euler discovered a relationship between the number of spaces, the
number of junctions and the number of lines in any network.
See if you can find this relationship yourself by drawing several networks
and recording information about each in a table, as below.

Number of spaces S	Number of junctions J	Number of lines L

If you are unable to find the relationship try adding the numbers of spaces to
the number of junctions for each network.

Could you draw a network with: (a) 2 spaces, 4 junctions and 5 lines?
66   (b) 3 spaces, 4 junctions and 5 lines?   (c) 2 spaces, 3 junctions and 5 lines?

For discussion

Here are some solid shapes you may have in your classroom.

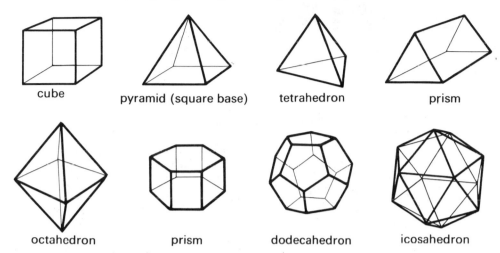

cube   pyramid (square base)   tetrahedron   prism

octahedron   prism   dodecahedron   icosahedron

Count the number of faces, the number of edges and the number of vertices on each of the shapes you have (use models). Record the results on a table.

Shape	Number of faces F	Number of vertices V	Number of edges E
cube	6	8	12

What do you notice?

There is a relationship between the faces, vertices and edges of shapes which is like the relationship between the spaces, junctions and lines of networks. Can you find this relationship?

Is it possible to make a shape with:
   (a) 6 faces, 6 vertices, 10 edges?
   (b) 7 faces, 10 vertices, 14 edges?
   (c) 6 faces, 8 vertices, 10 edges?
   (d) 9 faces, 9 vertices, 16 edges?
   (e) 3 faces, 4 vertices, 5 edges?

Draw sketches of the ones you think are possible. Try making one of them.   67

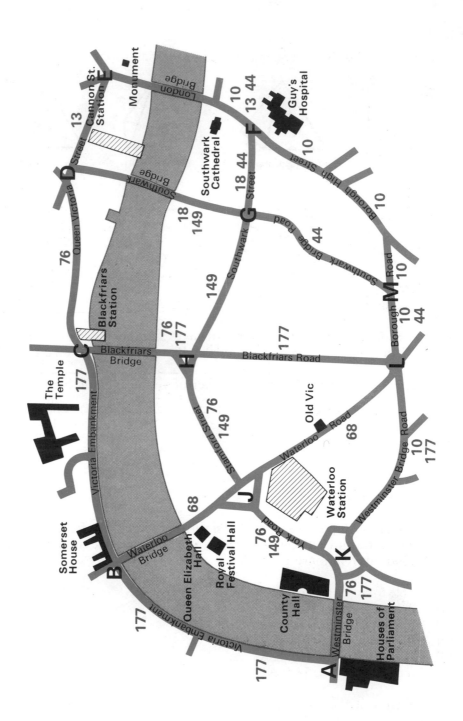

The Temple

Somerset House

Victoria Embankment

Waterloo Bridge

Queen Elizabeth Hall

Royal Festival Hall

County Hall

Houses of Parliament

Westminster Bridge

Victoria Embankment

Blackfriars Station

Blackfriars Bridge

Queen Victoria Street

Cannon St. Station

Monument

London Bridge

Southwark Bridge

Southwark Cathedral

Southwark Street

Guy's Hospital

Borough High Street

Southwark Bridge Road

Borough Road

Blackfriars Road

Stamford Street

Old Vic

Waterloo Road

Waterloo Station

York Road

Westminster Bridge Road

177 177 68 76 149 76 149 13 177 76 177 18 149 149 76 177 13 10 44 18 44 10 44 177 68 10 10 44 10 177 76 149 76 177

For discussion

On the opposite page there is a simplified map of some of the roads in central London.
The numbers by the sides of the roads are the service numbers of some of the buses which run along them. (Buses go both ways along each road.)
Important road junctions are labelled, using letters.

Find the Houses of Parliament on the map.
Find Guy's Hospital.
If you had to travel from the Houses of Parliament (junction **A**) to Guy's Hospital (junction **F**) what would be the service numbers of the buses you could use?
At which junction or junctions would you change?

The information about which services pass through the various junctions can be shown in a matrix, as below:

Junctions

	A	B	C	D	E	F	G	H	J	K	L	M
10	0	0	0	0	1	1	0	0	0	0	1	1
13	0	0	0	1	1	1	0	0	0	0	0	0
18	0	0	0	1	0	1	1	0	0	0	0	0
44												
68												
76												
149												
177												

Bus service numbers

Complete the matrix (Worksheet 29).

Find your route from the Houses of Parliament to Guy's Hospital, using the matrix.

Use the matrix to find a way of travelling from Blackfriars station (Junction **C**) to County Hall (junction **K**).
How would you make the journey if the 76 service was not running?

Use the matrix to find ways of travelling from Somerset House (junction **B**) to the Monument (junction **E**). Which way involves the fewest changes?

For discussion

Look at the map on the opposite page.

It shows some of the more important stations on the London underground railway system.

The key under the map shows the various lines.
Find the *Circle* line. Trace its path and name the stations through which it passes. Why do you think it has this name?

Trace the other lines in turn.
Find the important main line railway stations.

Which lines pass through: (a) Oxford Circus? (b) Baker Street? (c) Victoria? Through which junctions does the *Piccadilly* line pass?
How would you travel from Piccadilly Circus to Notting Hill Gate?

Record the information about which lines pass through which stations by completing the matrix shown below (Worksheet 30).

	Baker Street	Bank	Charing Cross	Earls Court	Edgware Road	Euston	Gloucester Road	Green Park	Holborn	King's Cross	Leicester Square	Liverpool Street	London Bridge	Marylebone	Moorgate	Notting Hill Gate	Old Street	Oxford Circus	Paddington	Piccadilly Circus	South Kensington	Tottenham Court Road	Victoria	Warren St	Waterloo
Bakerloo	1	0	1	0	1	0	0	0	0	0	0	0	0	1	0	0	0	1	1	1	0	0	0	0	1
Central	0	1	0	0	0	0	0	0	1	0	0	1	0	0	0	1	0	1	0	0	0	1	0	0	0
Circle	1	0	1	0	1	0	1	0	0	1	0	1	0	1	1	1	0	0	1	0	1	0	1	0	0
District																									
Metropolitan																									
Northern																									
Piccadilly																									
Victoria																									

Use the matrix to find a way of travelling from:
  (a) Piccadilly Circus to Notting Hill Gate.
  (b) King's Cross to Notting Hill Gate.
  (c) Charing Cross to Tottenham Court Road if the *Northern* line is closed.
  (d) Paddington to Piccadilly Circus if the *Bakerloo* line is closed.

What is the most number of changes you can make in going from Piccadilly Circus to Holborn without going through any junction twice?

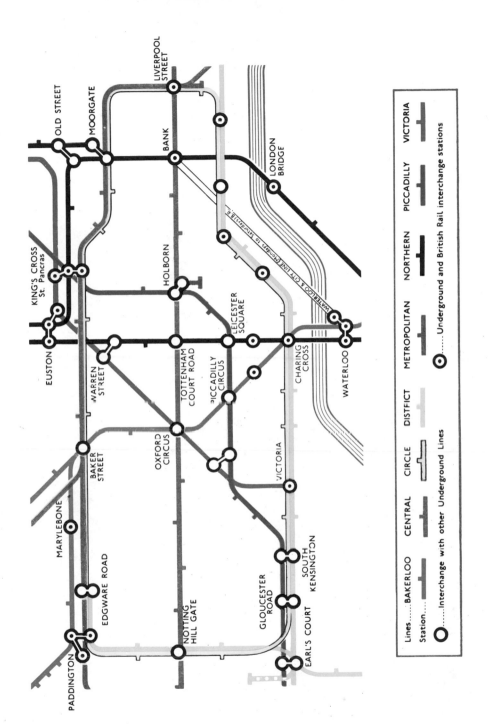

OLD STREET
MOORGATE
LIVERPOOL STREET
BANK
LONDON BRIDGE
KING'S CROSS St. Pancras
HOLBORN
LEICESTER SQUARE
CHARING CROSS
WATERLOO
WATERLOO & CITY LINE (Monday to Saturday) R.
EUSTON
WARREN STREET
TOTTENHAM COURT ROAD
PICCADILLY CIRCUS
VICTORIA
MARYLEBONE
BAKER STREET
OXFORD CIRCUS
EDGWARE ROAD
NOTTING HILL GATE
GLOUCESTER ROAD
SOUTH KENSINGTON
EARL'S COURT
PADDINGTON

Lines......BAKERLOO   CENTRAL   CIRCLE   DISTRICT   METROPOLITAN   NORTHERN   PICCADILLY   VICTORIA

Station......

O ......Interchange with other Underground Lines

⊙ ......Underground and British Rail interchange stations

RANDOM NUMBERS, AREA, VOLUME

For discussion

Is there any pattern to the way in
which the triangles in this square
have been coloured?

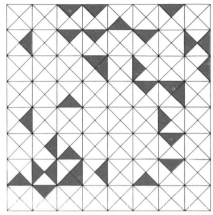

Is there any pattern to the ages,
occupation, sex, dress . . . of a
crowd of people entering a
London underground station
during the rush hour?

Premium Bond winning numbers are
produced by a computer called
ERNIE.
Here are some actual winning numbers.
Can you see any pattern in these?
Count the number of times each digit
appears. (Don't worry about the
letters.) What do you notice?

AK915057	EN646050	MF865250
HK340753	LT901575	EW113099
KW525399	QP946582	DZ749105
MS516038	SB850063	WL492725
RS534000	WK771289	TP766574
SW991905	CK642698	PB895623
SS438458	KF207014	JZ030270
VL191201	QF120394	HT516906
WF630013	TK168365	BN412272

When there is no pattern we say we are dealing with things at random.
The coloured triangles were chosen at random; the people at the
underground station are a random sample of London commuters; the Premium
Bond numbers are chosen at random. What about the lights on page 72?
A table of random numbers is given on the next page.

A table of random numbers

16 23	91 02	19 96	47 59	89 65	27 84	30 92	63 37	26 24	23 66
04 50	65 04	65 65	82 42	70 51	55 04	61 47	88 83	99 34	82 37
32 70	17 72	03 61	66 26	24 71	22 77	88 33	17 78	08 92	73 49
03 64	59 07	42 95	81 39	06 41	20 81	92 34	51 90	39 08	21 42
62 49	00 90	67 86	93 48	31 83	19 07	67 68	49 03	27 47	52 03
61 00	95 86	98 36	14 03	48 88	51 07	33 40	06 86	33 76	68 57
89 03	90 49	28 74	21 04	09 96	60 45	22 03	52 80	01 79	33 81
01 72	33 85	52 40	60 07	06 71	89 27	14 29	55 24	85 79	31 96
27 56	49 79	34 34	32 22	60 53	91 17	33 26	44 70	93 14	99 70
49 05	74 48	10 55	35 25	24 28	20 22	35 66	66 34	26 35	91 23
49 74	37 25	97 26	33 94	42 23	01 28	59 38	92 69	03 66	73 82
20 26	22 43	88 08	19 85	08 12	47 65	65 63	56 07	97 85	56 79
48 87	77 96	43 39	76 93	08 79	22 18	54 55	93 75	97 26	90 77
08 72	87 46	75 73	00 11	27 07	05 20	30 85	22 21	04 67	19 13
95 97	98 62	17 27	31 42	64 71	46 22	32 75	19 32	20 99	94 85
37 99	57 31	70 40	46 55	46 12	24 32	36 74	60 20	72 10	95 93
05 79	58 37	85 33	75 18	88 71	23 44	54 28	00 48	96 23	66 45
55 85	63 42	00 79	91 22	29 01	41 39	51 40	36 65	26 11	78 32
67 28	96 25	68 36	24 72	03 85	49 24	05 69	64 86	08 19	91 21
85 86	94 78	32 59	51 82	86 43	73 84	45 60	89 57	06 87	08 15
40 10	60 09	05 88	78 44	63 13	58 25	37 11	18 47	75 62	52 21
94 55	89 48	90 80	77 80	26 89	87 44	23 74	66 20	20 19	26 52
11 63	77 77	23 20	33 62	62 19	29 03	94 15	56 37	14 09	47 16
64 00	26 04	54 55	38 57	94 62	68 40	26 04	24 25	03 61	01 20
50 94	13 23	78 41	60 58	10 60	88 46	30 21	45 98	70 96	36 89
66 98	37 96	44 13	45 05	34 59	75 85	48 97	27 19	17 85	48 51
66 91	42 83	60 77	90 91	60 90	79 62	57 66	72 28	08 70	96 03
33 58	12 18	02 07	19 40	21 29	39 45	90 42	58 84	85 43	95 67
52 49	40 16	72 40	73 05	50 90	02 04	98 24	05 30	27 25	20 88
74 98	93 99	78 30	79 47	96 92	45 58	40 37	89 76	84 41	74 68
50 26	54 30	01 88	69 57	54 45	69 88	23 21	05 69	93 44	05 32
49 46	61 89	33 79	96 84	28 34	19 35	28 73	39 59	56 34	97 07
19 65	13 44	78 39	73 88	62 03	36 00	25 96	86 76	67 90	21 68
64 17	47 67	87 59	81 40	72 61	14 00	28 28	55 86	23 38	16 15
18 43	97 37	68 97	56 56	57 95	01 88	11 89	48 07	42 60	11 92

For discussion

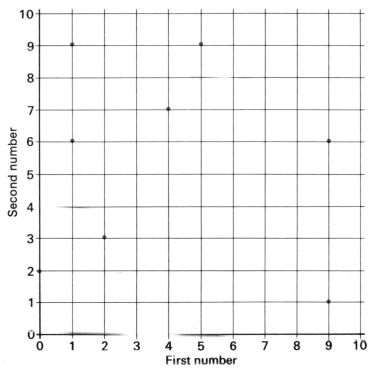

Look at the grid above.
A number of points have been marked using random numbers.

This is how it has been done.
The first two numbers in the table are 1 and 6.
Think of these as the number pair (1,6).
Find the mark for (1,6) above.

The next pair of numbers is (2,3). Find the mark for this.

A copy of the above grid, with the same points marked, is on Worksheet 31.
Label the point (1,6) with an *A* and the point (2,3) with a *B*.

A point on the worksheet is labelled *C*.
Is this the point for the next number pair in your random numbers?
Using *D, E, F, G* and *H* label, in order, the other five marked points.

Mark the points for the next five number pairs from the random numbers.
Label them *J, K, L, M* and *N*.

75

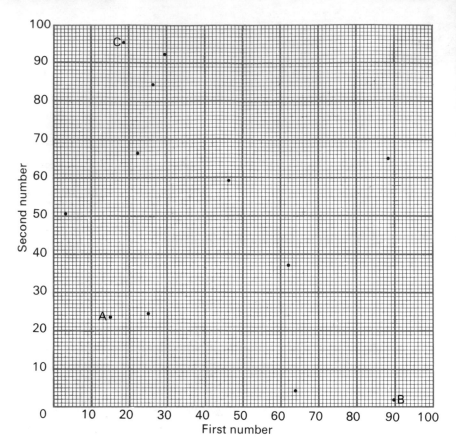

You need a sheet of centimetre graph paper, marked in tenths.
Mark and label two axes, as shown. Draw lines to complete a 10-cm square.

To obtain number pairs in which each number can go up to 99, *four* numbers
have to be chosen, in order, from the set of random numbers.
For example the first four random numbers, 1,6,2,3 give the pair (16,23).
The next four, 9,1,0,2, give the pair (91,2).
The third four, 1,9,9,6, give the pair (19,96).

These three pairs are marked on the grid above and are labelled **A, B** and **C.**

Twelve points have been marked on the grid by continuing in this way.
Check them to make sure they are correct.

Now use your own piece of graph paper.
Start from any place in the set of random numbers and mark the points for
100 pairs. Do not label them. Make sure you do not miss any of the random
numbers which come after your starting point.

What is the *area* of your 10-cm square grid?
How many *points* have you marked?

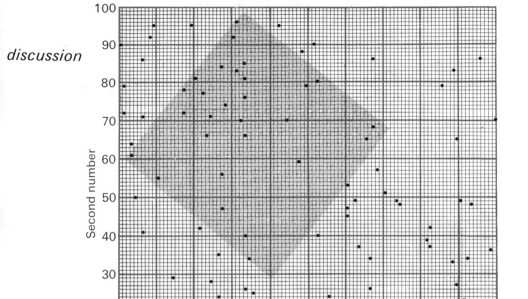

You need some tracing paper or acetate sheet.
Cut out a 5-cm square from your tracing paper. (This can easily be done by placing the tracing paper over your graph paper and marking it.)

Place your 5-cm square on your graph paper as shown, making sure that it does not go outside the 10-cm square.
Count the number of dots under the 5-cm square.
Move the 5-cm square to another position and again count the dots.
Move it again and count the dots.
Do this *ten* times recording your results.
Add your results and divide by 10 to get an average (mean) number of dots under a 5-cm square.
Record your results on a table as shown in the example below.

Side of square	Number of dots under square	Total	Average (mean)
5 cm	24, 32, 24, 26, 25, 26, 24, 21, 31, 26	259	25·9

What is the area of a 5-cm square?
What do you notice about the average (mean) number of dots and the area?

Exercises (It is advisable to work in groups.)

1. Cut from tracing paper, squares with sides 2 cm, 3 cm, 4 cm, 6 cm, 7 cm
    and 8 cm.
    For each square in turn, repeat the activity you have just done with the
    5-cm square.
    (Keep your squares, you will need them again.)
    Copy and complete this table.

Side of square	Number of dots under square	Total	Average	Area
2 cm				4 cm²
3 cm				9 cm²
4 cm				16 cm²
5 cm				25 cm²
6 cm				
7 cm				
8 cm				

What do you notice about the numbers in the *Average* and *Area* columns?
How does this dot counting method help you to find approximate areas?

2. Use the dot counting method to find the approximate area of:
    (a) a rectangle 6 cm long and 4 cm wide;
    (b) an equilateral triangle with side 8 cm;
    (c) an isosceles triangle with two sides 6 cm and one side 4 cm.

3. Use the dot counting method to find the approximate areas of some
    irregular shapes like these:

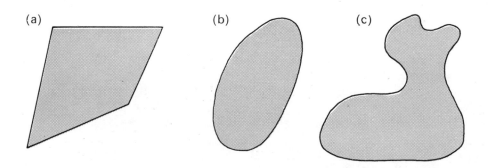

(a)   (b)   (c)

Check your approximate areas by some other method—for example,
square counting.

The area of a circle

For discussion

Use the squares of tracing paper
from pages 76 and 77.

Find the centre of each square and
draw a circle as shown.
(The diameter of each circle will be
the same as the side of the square.)

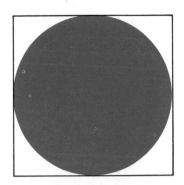

Is the area of the circle larger or smaller than the area of the square?
About what fraction of the area of the square is enclosed by the circle?

Take the 5-cm square and again place it on your 10-cm square grid.
Count the number of dots under the *circle*.
Move the circle and count the number of dots under it again.
Continue in this way until you have 10 results.
Record your results. Add the numbers and divide by 10 to find the average.

Do this with all your circles. (Again, you will find it easier to work in groups.)
Record the results on a table, as shown below (Worksheet 32).
Complete the table.

Diameter of circle	Number of points under circle	Total	Average (Area of circle)	Area of square
2 cm				4 cm²
3 cm				9 cm²
4 cm				16 cm²
5 cm				25 cm²
6 cm				36 cm²
7 cm				49 cm²
8 cm				64 cm²

What do you notice about the approximate area of each circle and the area of
the square surrounding it?
Do you agree that: the area of a circle is approximately three-quarters of the
area of the surrounding square?

This can be remembered as: approximate area is $\frac{3}{4}D^2$.

(*D* is the diameter of the circle and also the length of side of the square.)

79

Exercises

1. A circle has a diameter of 20 cm.
   What size square can be drawn round it so that its edges touch the circle?
   What is the area of the square?
   What is the approximate area of the circle?

2. Write down the approximate area of a circle with:
   (a) diameter 9 cm?   (b) diameter 16 cm?   (c) radius 10 cm?

Another way of finding the area of a circle

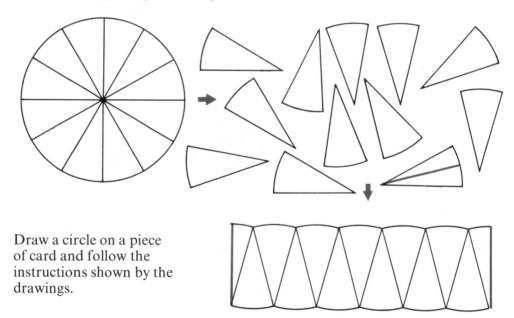

Draw a circle on a piece
of card and follow the
instructions shown by the
drawings.

The circumference of a circle is about 3 × diameter (or 6 × radius).

Look at the 'rectangle' you have made.
The two longer edges together make the circumference of the circle.
So each of the longer edges is 3 × radius.
The 'width' of the rectangle is approximately the radius of the circle.
So the area of the rectangle is approximately (3 × radius) × (radius).
This can be written as 3 × radius × radius or 3 × (radius)².
Is this the same as $\frac{3}{4}D^2$?

Note: the exact area of a circle is given by: Area = πr^2
           where $\pi \simeq 3\cdot14$ or $3\frac{1}{7}$.

Exercise

Find the area of the coloured shape:

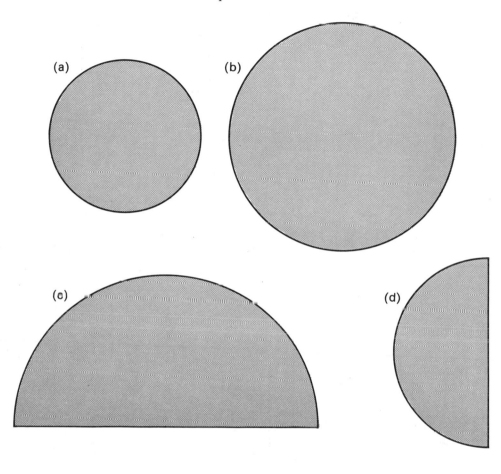

(a)

(b)

(c)

(d)

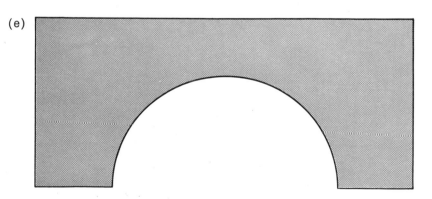

(e)

81

6

The volume of a prism

For discussion

You need 1-cm squared paper and plenty of 1-cm cubes.

On your squared paper mark six squares, as shown.

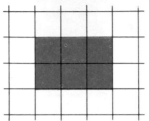

What is the area of the coloured part?
Place a cube on each square.
What is the total volume of the cubes used?

Put in a second layer of cubes.
What is the total volume of the cubes now?

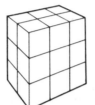

What will be the volume with a third layer?
a fourth layer?

The shape you build in this way, based
on a rectangle, is a rectangular prism or
cuboid.

Now mark 14 squares as shown
and cover each square with a cube.
What is the volume of your shape?

Add another layer of the same number of
cubes. What is the volume now?

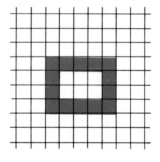

What will the volume be when there are
seven layers altogether? How high
is the shape?

What will the volume be when the shape
is   (a) 8 cm high?   (b) 10 cm high?

Can you see a way of finding the
volume of shapes which are built up in
this way?

This shape is also a prism.

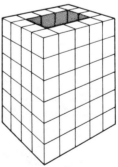

Starting with any shapes you choose on your squared paper make other prisms
and find their volumes.

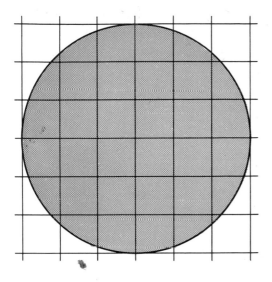

A circle is drawn on 1-cm squares.
What is the area of the circle?

If this circle were covered with 1-cm cubes how many would be needed? (Assume that you can cut up the centimetre cubes.)
This one-centimetre layer will give you a cylinder of height one centimetre.
What is the volume of the cylinder?

A cylinder can be thought of as a circular prism, as it is built up in the same way as the prisms on the previous page.

How many cubes would be required for 2 layers? 3 layers?...
What is the volume of a cylinder of diameter 6 cm and height:
(a) 5 cm?   (b) 7 cm?   (c) 10 cm?

Any shape which can be built up in the way described on this and the previous page is called a prism.
Here are some examples of prisms.

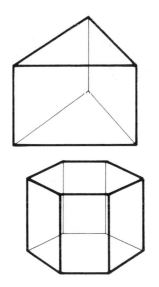

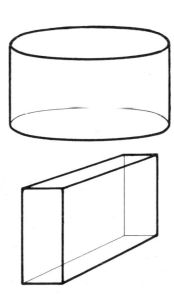

83

Exercises

1. What is the volume of a prism built on a triangle of area 27 cm² if its height is 8 cm?

2. What is the volume of a prism of height 13 cm and built on a hexagon of area 24 cm²?

3. Find the volume of each of the following shapes.

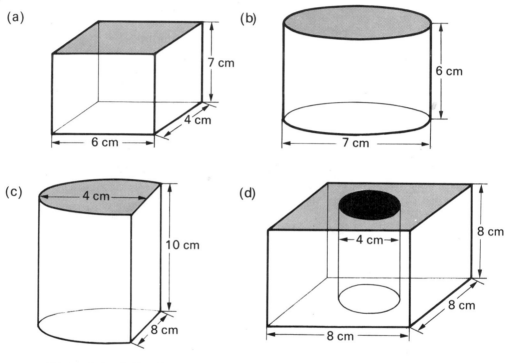

(a) 7 cm 4 cm 6 cm

(b) 6 cm 7 cm

(c) 4 cm 10 cm 8 cm

(d) 4 cm 8 cm 8 cm 8 cm

4. Which of the following are prisms?

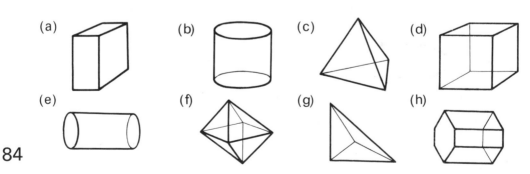

(a) (b) (c) (d)

(e) (f) (g) (h)

84

STATISTICS

For discussion

The two tables below are based on similar tables from the magazine *Which?*.
They give information regarding 'desirable' mass according to height and
type of body frame.

The masses include indoor clothes. To get a 'fully-stripped' mass, 5 kg
should be taken off for a man and 3 kg for a woman.

MEN

Height without shoes cm	Body frame		
	Small kg	Medium kg	Large kg
160	58	63	68
162·5	59	64	70
165	61	66	72
167·5	63	68	74
170	65	70	76
172·5	67	72	78
175	70	74	80
177·5	71	76	82
180	73	78	84
182·5	74	80	87
185	77	83	89
187·5	78	85	91
190	80	87	93

WOMEN

Height without shoes cm	Body frame		
	Small kg	Medium kg	Large kg
150	49	53	59
152·5	49	54	60
155	52	56	61
157·5	53	58	63
160	54	59	65
162·5	56	62	67
165	58	64	68
167·5	60	65	70
170	62	67	72
172·5	64	69	74
175	66	71	77
177·5	68	73	79
180	69	74	82

Find your height in the above tables.
Decide whether you have a small, medium or large body frame.
Are you the mass suggested for your height?

Suggest possible masses for the different size frames for:
(a) a 155 cm man   (b) a 145 cm woman   (c) a 185 cm woman.

Compare the masses given for a 165 cm man and a 165 cm woman.
Can you suggest reasons for the difference?

A 165 cm woman who has a mass of 63 kg could be:
'medium frame, normal mass'; 'small framed and fat'; 'large framed and
thin'.
Give several descriptions of a 180 cm man who is 79 kg.

85

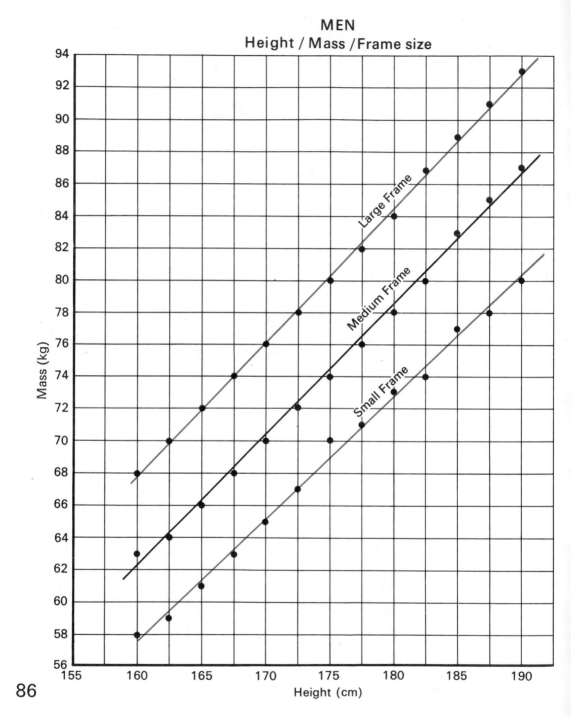

MEN
Height / Mass / Frame size

On the opposite page you can see that the
information given in the table for men has been
shown by a graph.

A line has been drawn to show the approximate
trend of each of the different frame sizes.
(The graph is reproduced on Worksheet 33.)

In the same way, on Worksheet 34, show the
information from the table for women.
Show the approximate trend of each frame size
by a straight line.

You now have on Worksheet 33 and 34 the
information for men and for women.

Now collect the heights (without shoes) and masses
(with clothes) of each pupil in your class.
Put the height and mass information on Worksheet
33 or 34, whichever is appropriate, representing
each person by a coloured dot.
Comment on your results in relation to what *Which?*
describes as 'desirable' mass according to frame size.
What can you say about people:
   (a) above the lines?   (b) below the lines?

Collect similar information from as many adults as
possible—say about 30 or 40
Record this information on the appropriate graph on
Worksheet 33 or 34, using a different colour for these dots.
Comment on these results in relation to:
   (a) the *Which?* results;   (b) your class results.

Exercises

Choose one or two of the following exercises. Collect the information required. Show the information by graphs and comment on the results you obtain.

1. From your local library or H.M.S.O. find out the changes in population over the last hundred years of your town or parish. Ten yearly intervals will be sufficient to show changes.
   Can you account for the changes?
   Can you suggest the possible population changes in the next 30 years?

2. Count how many vehicles pass you at a point on a busy road during an hour (or some other suitable period of time).
   Classify them according to type (e.g. make, size, colour, year, registration letters, etc.).

3. Take any newspaper and make a table showing about how many columns are allocated to: (a) news; (b) features; (c) advertisements; (d) sport; (e) pictures; (f) other items.
   Do this for another newspaper and, using graphs, compare the results.
   What connection is there between advertising space and the sales of a newspaper?

4. Over a period of several weeks compare the number of goals scored in each of the four divisions of the Football League in England.
   Can you explain any differences you might find?

5. Obtain information about the *monthly* rainfall in your area during the last year.
   Compare your results with those of another area or town.

   What effect does rainfall have on: (a) holiday visitors? (b) crops grown in your area? (c) sport played in your area? (d) any other activity or occupation of people in your area?

6. By 'window shopping' find the prices of a particular item of food in different shops.
   Can you account for the different prices? Is it true that if one item of food is cheaper in a shop, then most items will be? Are there certain foods which always seem to be 'on offer'? Why?

Correlation

For discussion

On Worksheet 35 you will find some graph paper labelled like that opposite.

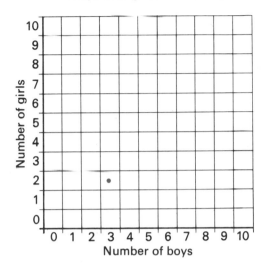

Boys and girls in a family

How many children are there in your family, including yourself?
How many of these are boys? How many are girls?
This information can be recorded by putting a dot in one of the squares on the graph.
For example: If there are five children in the family and 3 are boys and 2 are girls, a dot would be put in the square for 3 boys and 2 girls, as shown above. (The dot can be put anywhere in the square.)
Find out from each of 100 pupils in your school how many boys and girls there are in their family. Remind them to include themselves. (Be careful not to ask two pupils from the same family.)
Record the information for *each* child with a dot on your graph.

> When information is recorded in this way, the graph produced is called a
> scattergram

Count the number of dots in each square on your scattergram.
Record the number for each square in the corresponding square on Worksheet 36. The information is now in a matrix form.

Now make a scattergram and a matrix for boys and girls in the families of the *parents* of the pupils in your class and others of the same age group (100 families altogether). Use Worksheets 37 and 38.

89

Exercises

You need the scattergrams and matrices on Worksheets 35, 36, 37 and 38.

1. Look at the two scattergrams (Worksheets 35 and 37).
   Pick out and colour the squares in which the number of boys is the same as the number of girls.
   Also pick out and colour (using different colours) the squares in which there are: (a) more boys than girls;   (b) more girls than boys.
   What do you notice?

2. Look at the matrix for the pupils in your school (Worksheet 36).
   Use a coloured pencil to shade all the squares showing families with 3 children.
   How many families of 3 children are there?
   How many families of 2 children?
   How many 'only child' families?
   What is the most common size of family? What kind of average is this?

3. Look at the matrix for parents and others of about their age (Worksheet 38).
   How many families are there of: 1 child?   2 children?   3 children?...
   Compare this with the results from Exercise 2.
   Were your parents' families larger or smaller than present-day families.
   Can you think of any reasons for this?

4.   1   4   6   4   1

   What has this row of Pascal's triangle to do with the number of boys and girls in a family of four children?

   Look at the number of families with four children on the matrix on Worksheet 36.
   How many are there?
   Write the number of these which are:
   (a) all boys; (b) all girls; (c) 3 boys and 1 girl; (d) 3 girls and 1 boy; (e) 2 boys and 2 girls.
   How do these results compare with those shown in Pascal's triangle?

90   Compare other size families with the corresponding rows in Pascal's triangle.

For discussion

The tallest people wear the largest shoes

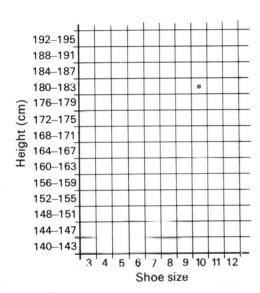

Collect information from *either* 100 men *or* 100 women.
Include your own 4th year and 5th year.

Ask each person their height and shoe size.
Enter the information on Worksheet 39 by putting a dot in the correct square for each person.
An example: a person with shoes of size 10 and height 181 cm would be entered as shown.
(For shoe sizes given in halves go to the next whole size above: e.g. size 4½ would be called size 5.)

Look at the scattergram you have drawn.
Do the dots seem to be arranged in any particular pattern.
Would you say it is true that, in general, *the taller a person, the larger the shoes he wears?*

The larger the car (i.e. its engine size), the smaller the number of kilometres per litre

Collect information about the engine size and petrol consumption of a number of different cars.
Record your findings by a scattergram.

What do you notice about the way the dots are arranged on your scattergram this time?
Do you think that, in general, it is true to say *the larger the engine size the smaller the number of kilometres per litre?*

91

For discussion

Look at these three scattergrams.

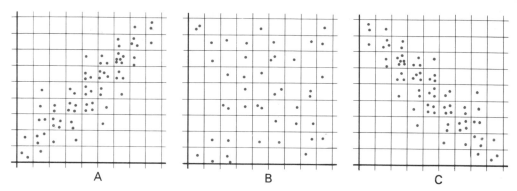

Which of the three scattergrams has the same kind of pattern as the shoe-size/height scattergram you drew?

Which has the same kind of pattern as your engine-size/kilometres per litre scattergram?

Which of the three patterns do you think you would get if you drew a scattergram for:

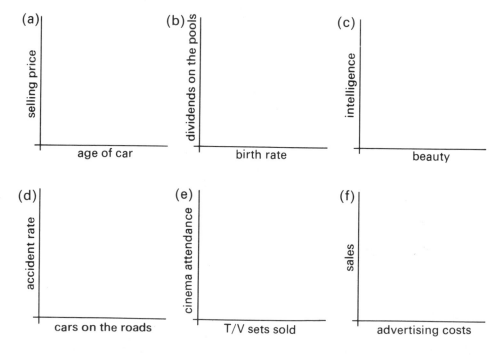

Arrangements in a row

WIN A FREE HOLIDAY FOR TWO AT CARLYPONT HOLIDAY CAMP

Here's all you have to do.
Read the items carefully and place them in your order of importance for a happy holiday. If you think D is the most important you will write D in the 1st space and so on.

Complete this sentence:
I prefer Holiday Camps to other kinds of holiday because:- _ _ _ _ _ _ _ _ _

A Heated swimming pool
B Evening cabaret
C Indoor games room
D Plenty of good food
E Sandy beach with safe sea swimming.

1st	2nd	3rd	4th	5th

Name _ _ _ _ _ _ _ _ _
Address _ _ _ _ _ _ _ _ _

Decide on the order in which you would place the letters and write them on a piece of paper.

On the blackboard make a list of the orders chosen by the members of your class. Are any of the orders the same?

How many *different* orders are there on the list?

How many different orders do you think you could have altogether?

How many different orders can you have if you have written
  (a) **ABCD** in the first four places?   (b) **ABC** in the first three places?
  (c) **AB** in the first two places?   (d) **A** in the first place?

Can you now say how many different orders there are altogether?

Why do you think you were asked to complete a sentence in the competition?

Collect details of other competitions like the one above.
Find the number of possible orders for each.

93

For discussion

Here is another way of finding the number of orders in which **A,B,C,D** and **E** can be put in a row.

Five large cards marked **A, B, C, D** and **E** for the five choices in the competition are needed.

| A | B | C | D | E |

Five members of your class each has one of these cards and brings it to the front when required.

Suppose there had been only two choices, say **A** and **B**.
In how many orders can they be put?
Let the two pupils with **A** and **B** stand in the two different orders.

Now include **C** so that you now have three choices **A, B** and **C**. With **A** and **B** standing in the first way, **C** can stand in three positions, as shown.

But **A** and **B** might be standing in the second way.
In how many places can **C** stand now?
Make a list of all the possible orders for **A, B** and **C**.

Now include the person with the card **D**.
Choose one of your orders for **A, B** and **C**, say
In how many places can **D** stand?

| C | A | B |

In how many places can **D** stand for each order of **A, B** and **C**?
How many different orders does this give for **A, B, C** and **D**?
By using the same method find the total number of different orders for the five items **A, B, C, D** and **E**.

Exercises

Choose some of the exercises from the next two pages.

1.
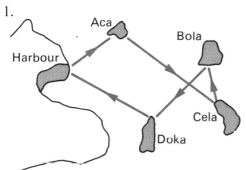

The captain of a patrol boat has to make daily visits to each of the four islands Aca, Bola, Cela and Doka.

On the first day he visits the islands in the order shown by the arrows—Aca, Cela, Bola, Doka.

This order can be written **ACBD.**

He wants to visit the islands in a different order each day.
Write out all the possible different orders.

2. Write down as many different 3-digit numbers as you can using 1, 2 and 3 each time.
   How many of your numbers are odd?
   How many are even?
   Why are there more odd numbers than even numbers?
   How many of your numbers can be divided exactly by: (a) 3? (b) 6?

3. Jim, Tony, Mary and Ruth are at the cinema.
   They are to sit in the four seats shown (1, 2, 3 and 4).
   In how many different ways can they arrange themselves?
   If Mary wishes to sit by Tony and Ruth wishes to sit by Jim, in how many different ways can they sit?

4.

John, Peter, Marilyn and Susan have booked four seats on a coach.

Each of the girls wishes to sit by a boy. In how many different ways can they arrange themselves?

If Susan wishes to sit with John, and Marilyn with Peter, in how many ways can they arrange themselves?

5. A five-a-side soccer team are having their photograph taken.

   In how many different ways can the team stand so that the captain is in the middle?

6.

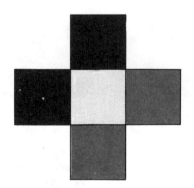

In how many different ways can you colour this shape using not more than 3 colours?

Rule:
   Two squares touching along an edge must not be the same colour.

How many different ways are there if the centre square is always black?

For discussion

SIMPLE SIX																												
FORECAST ALL SIX MATCHES MARK 12X																												
1	Tottenham	West Ham																										
2	Newcastle	Arsenal																										
3	Liverpool	Man. Utd.																										
4	Wolves	Everton																										
5	Charlton	Hull																										
6	Exeter	Southend																										
STAKE PER COLUMN MIN 1p MAX 20p																												

What is meant by 'MARK 1 2 X'?
What do you understand by 'STAKE PER COLUMN' and 'MIN 1p, MAX 20p'?
To win on this Pool you have to forecast all six results correctly.

How many *different* columns do you think you would have to fill in to make sure of getting the all-correct one?

If there was only one match to forecast it could be 1, 2 or X.

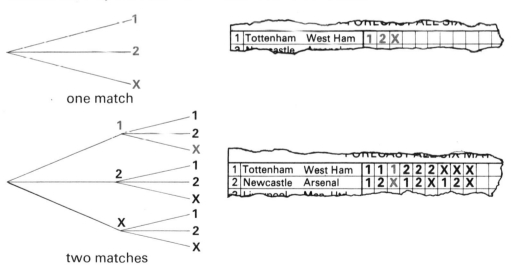

one match

two matches

Can you see how the columns have been filled in using the diagram (tree) on the left?

How many columns are there?

7

1	Tottenham	West Ham	1	1	1	1	1	1	1	1	1	2	2	2	2	2	2	2	2	2	X	X	X	X	X	X	X	X	X
2	Newcastle	Arsenal	1	1	1	2	2	2	X	X	X	1	1	1	2	2	2	X	X	X	1	1	1	2	2	2	X	X	X
3	Liverpool	Man. Utd.	1	2	X	1	2	X	1	2	X	1	2	X	1	2	X	1	2	X	1	2	X	1	2	X	1	2	X
4	Wolves	Everton																											

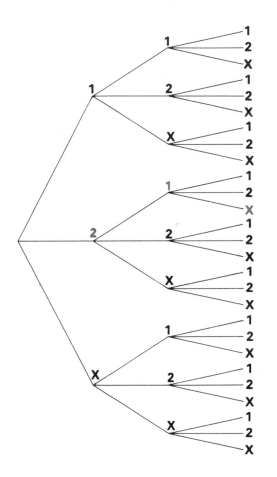

Can you see how the columns have been completed using the 'tree' on the left?

In how many *different* ways can the coupon be filled in for three matches?

Can you see a way of finding all the different 'three match' columns from the 'two match' columns on the previous page?

How many *different* columns will there be for four matches? for five matches? for six matches?
Complete the table.

Number of matches	Number of different columns
1	3
2	9
3	
4	
5	
6	

Think of another way of writing the 'Number of different columns'. (*Note:* at each junction on the tree there are three choices. This is a 3-state system). Use this other way to state the number of columns required for 20 matches. (Don't work it out unless you wish to, or have a calculating machine.)

If you stake the minimum amount per column, what will it cost to be sure of winning the 'Simple Six'?

PLANS AND MAPS

For discussion

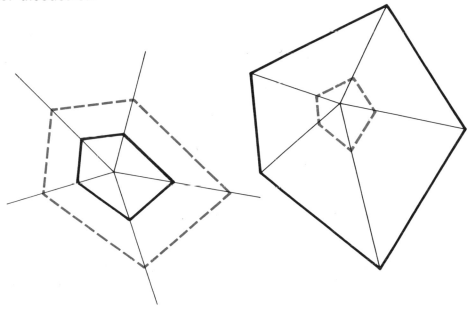

In Book 3 you saw how a shape could be made larger or smaller by using the *ray* method.
Look at the black shapes above.
Discuss how the coloured shapes have been obtained using the ray method.

On a large sheet of paper draw any shape.
Use the ray method to draw a similar shape with edges:
    (a) twice as long;
    (b) three times as long;
    (c) half as long.

Sometimes the shape we wish to make smaller is too large to be drawn on paper in the first place.
To draw the plan of a bungalow full size we would require a very large piece of paper! We have to make a scale drawing.
When such a plan is needed we have to decide on a convenient scale to enable us to fit the drawing on to a piece of paper.

Collect some drawings and maps which have a scale given on them.

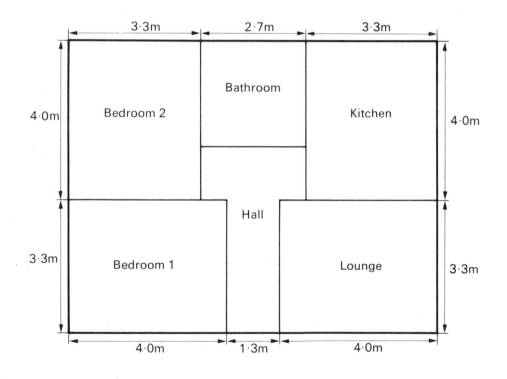

For discussion

What is meant by the following?

Find out what scales are used for these:

Ordnance survey maps.
Maps in your school atlas.
The official plans of your school or another building.

On the facing page is a simplified plan of a bungalow.
Use a convenient scale to draw this on squared paper.
If it is more interesting to draw a plan of the ground floor of your own house,
do so.

Each of the following has been drawn to scale and has one measurement
marked.
Find the scale used in each case and on a *sketch* in your own book, write the
measurements not shown.

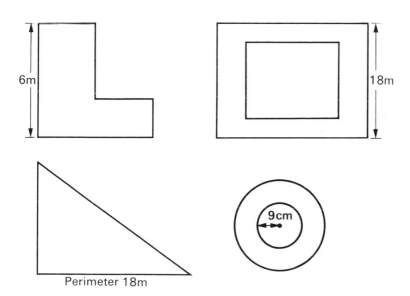

Perimeter 18m

101

Surveying a field

There are a number of ways of making a scale drawing of a field or other large area. One of these, called a plane table survey, is based on a kind of ray method. There are expensive pieces of equipment for doing this accurately, but it is possible to do it with reasonable accuracy using equipment from your classroom.

You need: a flat table (plane table), a straight edge with sights (alidade), a ruler, some drawing pins, and a large sheet of drawing paper.

The alidade (straight edge with sights) can be made with a ruler and two panel pins.

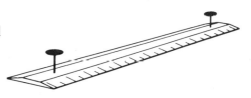

Before using your equipment to make a scale drawing of the large area make a sketch of the area.

On your sketch mark a number of landmarks that are at the edge of the field. These landmarks should give a good indication of the shape of the area. (Landmarks at corners are particularly useful—put in some posts if there are none.) Label each landmark on your sketch.

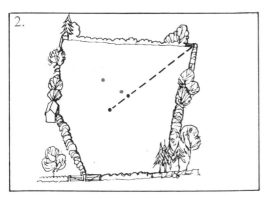

You now have to place two pegs in the field. It is important that these are *not* in line with any of your landmarks.
The position of the black pegs is not satisfactory—can you see why? The position of the blue pegs would be satisfactory.
Remembering this, place your two pegs ten metres apart in the middle of the field.

Mark the approximate positions of the pegs on your sketch. Label them *P* and *Q*. Decide on a suitable scale so that the drawing will fit on to your large sheet of paper.

Pin your large sheet of paper to the table. Near the centre of your paper mark two points for pegs *P* and *Q* according to the scale you have decided on.

Place the table over peg *P*. Use your alidade to line up the mark *Q* on the paper with peg *Q* on the field, by turning the table. Secure the table.

Place one edge of your alidade against *P* on your paper. Line up one of the landmarks. Draw a feint line to the edge of your paper. Do this for each landmark in turn.

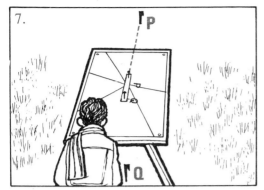

Now move the table to be over peg Q on the field. Line up the mark P on your paper with peg P on the field by turning the table. Secure the table.

Place one edge of your alidade against Q on your paper. Line up each of the landmarks in turn, drawing a feint line for each. Mark each of the landmarks on your paper.

Your piece of paper could now look something like this:

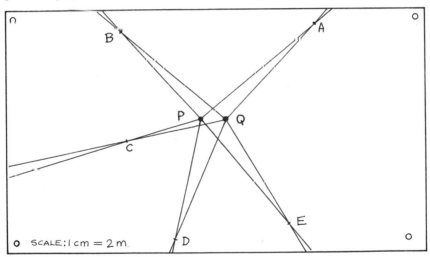

If the field has straight edges then the landmarks can be joined by straight lines to give a scale drawing of the area.
Mark the scale at the bottom of your drawing.
Measure the distance between two landmarks and check on your drawing to see how accurate it is.
If some of the edges are very curved, try to decide on a method of drawing them fairly accurately.

For discussion

The map on the opposite page is part of a larger sheet produced by the Ordnance Survey.

On this sheet the following statements appear:

   1 centimetre on the map represents 0·5 kilometres

   1 kilometre is represented by 2 centimetres on the map

   SCALE   1 : 50,000

Which of these three ways of stating the scale do you find the easiest to understand?

How would you state the scale using centimetres and metres?

When you find distances from a map you can either
   (a) measure the direct distance ('as the crow flies'), or
   (b) measure the distance by road or rail.

To find the distance by road or rail you need to use a piece of thin string (or thread) or a map measurer.

Exercises

1. Find the direct distance between Shalford station and Guildford station. What is the distance by rail between these two stations?

2. Find the length of the tunnel on the railway line between Shalford and Guildford.

3. Find the distance by road from the crossroads at Bramley to the intersection of A25 and A246.
    How far is this distance as the crow flies?

4. What is the greatest height shown on the map?
    Where is it?

5. How would you describe the position of:
    (a) the intersection of A246 and A25?
    (b) the station at Shalford?
    (c) Guildford Cathedral?

106

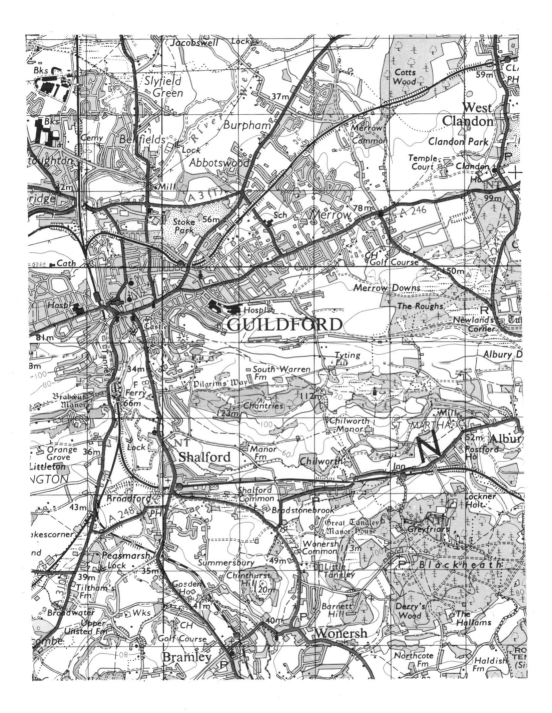

The direct distance between the Conger Rocks (in the Exe estuary) and the station at Exmouth is 2 kilometres (2000 metres).
What is the scale of this map? Can you give the scale in more than one way?

What is the shortest distance, by path and road, from the Coastguard Lookout at Orcombe Point to Exmouth Hospital?
How far is this as the crow flies?

What is the width of the Exe, at low water, opposite The Maer?

108

For discussion

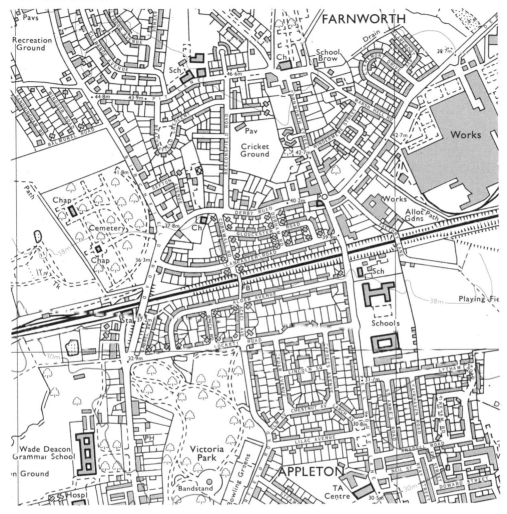

The scale of this map is given as: 1 : 10,000.
Do you agree that this could be given as:
   1 centimetre on the map represents 100 metres?

List the roads you would go along to get from the Bandstand in Victoria
Park to the Post Office.
What is the length of your route? Is it the shortest route?
What is the distance as the crow flies?

109

Exercises

1. From the work which you did on page 53 you estimated your walking speed. Use this speed to estimate how long it would take you to walk from:

   (a) the station at Shalford to the station at Bramley (Map on page 107).

   (b) Maer Farm to Straight Point (Map on page 108).

   (c) the Bandstand in Victoria Park to the Pavilion on the Cricket Ground.

2. (a) Plan a walk, lasting about two hours and returning to your starting point, using the map on page 108.

   (b) Plan a walk, lasting about five hours and returning to your starting point, using the map on page 107.

For discussion

You may remember, from the work you did in Book 2, that areas of fields, parks, football pitches, etc., are measured in hectares.

1 hectare = 10,000 m².

A square field, each of whose edges is 100 metres, has an area of 1 hectare.

It might be helpful to peg out such a square on your sports field. It will give you an idea of the size of a hectare.

Find some information about the areas, in hectares, of some of the open spaces in your town.

Exercises

3. Find, in hectares, the area of one or more of the following:
   (a) the cricket field shown on page 109.
   (b) the land between the railway line and the coast on page 108.
   (c) the Roughs (coloured green) on page 107.
   (d) the cemetery on page 109.
   (e) Liverton Copse on page 108.

For discussion

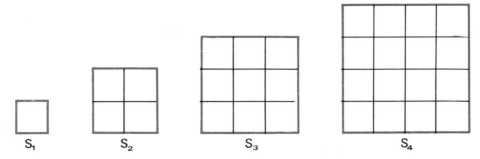

How do the coloured squares grow?
What can you say about (a) the perimeters (b) the areas of the squares?

Make up a table of areas and perimeters for S_1, S_2, S_3, S_4, . . .
(Think of the length of a side of the small square as one unit.)
How do the perimeters and the areas grow?

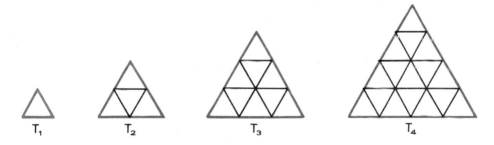

How do the triangles grow? What can you say about their areas?
What is the perimeter of each?

Make up a table of areas and perimeters for T_1, T_2, T_3, T_4, . . .
How do the perimeters and areas grow?

How do you think areas grow in relation to length?

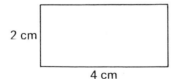

What is the area of this rectangle?

What would be the area of the rectangle if the dimensions were doubled?

What would be the dimensions of a similar rectangle whose area is 72 cm²?   **111**

For discussion

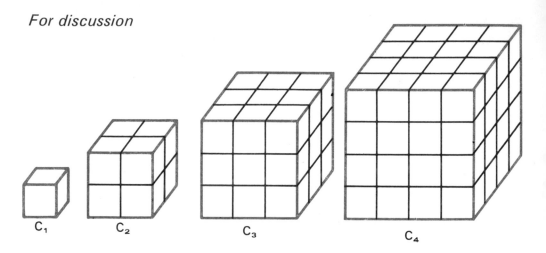

How do the cubes grow?
How many of C_1 are there in each?
How do the total edge lengths grow?
How do the surface areas grow?
Make up a table to show this information for C_1, C_2, C_3, C_4, . . .

Fasten small balls (marbles, polystyrene) together to make the shapes shown.
You will have to find a way of holding the bottom layer together.
Count the number of balls in each shape.
How do the numbers grow?
Find these numbers in Pascall's triangle (page 42).
What do you think the next number will be? And the next?

How do you think volumes grow in relation to length?

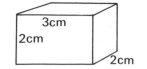

What is the volume of this cuboid?
What would be the volume if the dimensions
were (a) doubled? (b) trebled?

112

Exercises

1.

A kitchen floor has to be tiled.
The area to be tiled is a rectangle
of length 4·5 m and width 3 m.

How many 30-cm square tiles will you
need?

The shop only stocks 15-cm square
tiles.
How many will you need?

2.

Milk is delivered in either bottles
or cartons, each holding one
litre.

How much would the bottle or carton
hold if the dimensions were doubled?

3.

Collect some model cars from
younger brothers or friends.

Also collect some brochures from
garages about the same vehicles.

Are the toys exact scale models of
the actual cars?

To what scale have they been made? **113**

USING FORMULAE

Impedance of loudspeaker
$$Z_T = R + j\omega L + \frac{(G')^2}{j\omega m}$$

Thrust
$$F = \lambda C_d C_v A_t p_c \Gamma \sqrt{\frac{2\gamma}{\gamma-1}\left(\frac{X_e}{1+X_e}\right)} + A_e(p_e$$

Depth of field
$$\delta l_1 + \delta l_2 = \frac{2xDA}{A^2 - x^2}$$

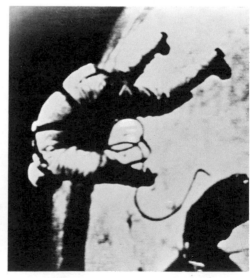

Energy to escape gravitational field
$$E = gr$$

A peg game

For discussion

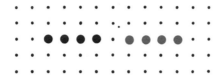

You need a piece of pegboard and pegs of two colours. (Blue pegs and black pegs will be used here.)
Place four pegs of each colour in a row on the pegboard, leaving one hole between them as shown above.

The object of the game (which was invented by a French mathematician called Lucas) is to reverse the positions of the pegs so that they end up like this:

Here are the rules of the game.
1. Use only the holes you started with.
2. Blue pegs can only be moved to the left, black pegs can only be moved to the right.
3. A peg can be moved into an empty hole if the hole is immediately in front of it.
4. A peg can jump *one* peg of the other colour provided it can land in an empty hole.

To make the rules clear, here are the first four moves of someone's game.

Begin · · ● ● ● ● · ● ● ● ● · ·	Make these moves yourself on your pegboard.
1st move · · ● ● ● ● ● · ● ● ● · ·	
2nd move · · ● ● ● · ● ● ● ● · ·	Can you see why these moves will not succeed?
3rd move · · ● ● ● ● · ● ● ● · ·	
4th move · · ● ● · ● ● ● ● ● · ·	Try the game yourself.

115

This game is quite difficult and you may not have succeeded in doing it.
One way to tackle a problem is to try a more simple one which is like it.
So try the game with just one peg of each colour.

Here is one way you may have found of making the moves (starting with the blue peg).

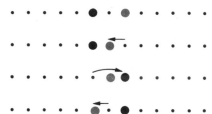

You notice that the blue peg is moved first, then the black peg and finally the blue peg.
Using **B** for blue and **K** for black, these moves could be recorded as **BKB**.

Now try the game with two pegs of each colour. (Start with a blue peg.)

How many moves does it take?
Record the moves using the letters **B** and **K**.

Now try the game using three pegs of each colour.

How many moves does it take?
Record the moves using the letters **B** and **K**.

Look carefully at the records of your moves (using **B** and **K**).
Do you notice any pattern?

What do you think would be the moves for four pegs of each colour? Write it down.
Try it to see whether it works.

Did it work?
If not look at your records to see whether you can find a pattern which does work.

Do you think you can write down the moves for five pegs of each colour?
116 If so, write it down and try it.

How many moves?

When you played the game with one peg of each colour, how many moves did you take?
How many did you take when you played with:
   2 of each colour?   3 of each colour?   4 of each colour?

These numbers can be shown in a table like the one below.

Number of pegs of each colour	Number of moves
1 ⟶	3
2 ⟶	
3 ⟶	
4 ⟶	

Copy and complete the table.
What do you notice?
Can you say how many moves will be needed for five pegs of each colour?

A way of showing how the number of moves is related to the number of pegs of each colour has been worked out. It is:
$$\text{moves} = \text{pegs} \times (\text{pegs} + 2)$$
Using *m* for the number of moves and *p* for the number of pegs, this statement can be written more shortly as:
$$m = p \times (p + 2)$$
Note: a statement such as this is often called a formula.

This is how the formula is used.
If you want to know the number of moves for 3 pegs of each colour then you put 3 in place of the *p* in the formula, $m = p \times (p + 2)$.

This gives $m = 3 \times (3 + 2)$
$$= 15$$

Does this agree with the result in your table?
Use the formula to find the number of moves for:
   (a) 1 peg,   (b) 2 pegs,   (c) 3 pegs,   of each colour.
Do the results agree with those in your table?

Now use the formula to find the number of moves for:
   (a) 5 pegs,   (b) 7 pegs, (c) 10 pegs,   (d) 19 pegs, of each colour.

You might try the puzzle with 10 pegs of each colour.   **117**

Stopping distances

For discussion

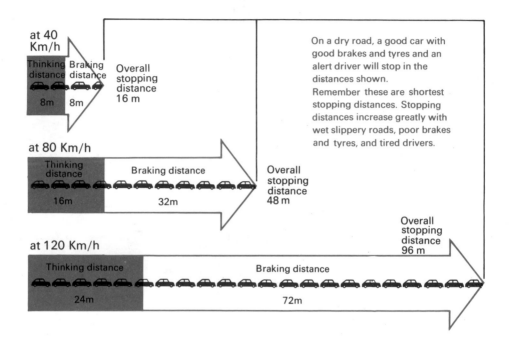

at 40 Km/h

Thinking distance | Braking distance

8m | 8m

Overall stopping distance 16 m

On a dry road, a good car with good brakes and tyres and an alert driver will stop in the distances shown.
Remember these are shortest stopping distances. Stopping distances increase greatly with wet slippery roads, poor brakes and tyres, and tired drivers.

at 80 Km/h

Thinking distance — 16m

Braking distance — 32m

Overall stopping distance 48 m

at 120 Km/h

Thinking distance — 24m

Braking distance — 72m

Overall stopping distance 96 m

This diagram, amended from The Highway Code, gives the shortest stopping distances for cars travelling at various speeds.
What do you understand by the diagram?

What is meant by *thinking distance?* What is meant by *braking distance?*
What is meant by *overall stopping distance?*
Why is the thinking distance more for 80 km/h than for 40 km/h?

What is the *thinking distance* for (a) 40 km/h? (b) 80 km/h?
What is the *braking distance* for (a) 40 km/h? (b) 80 km/h?
What is the *overall stopping distance* for (a) 40 km/h? (b) 80 km/h?
How much longer is the *overall stopping distance* for 80 km/h than for 40 km/h?

What is the *overall stopping distance* for 120 km/h?
Think of a distance in the school grounds that is about the same as this.

Here is a table giving the *overall stopping distances* (in metres) for various *speeds* (in km/h).

Speed (km/h)		Overall stopping distance (metres)
40	$\longrightarrow$	16
60	$\longrightarrow$	30
80	$\longrightarrow$	48
100	$\longrightarrow$	70
120	$\longrightarrow$	96

A statement which gives the approximate relation between speed and overall stopping distance is:

$$\text{distance} = \frac{\text{speed}}{10} \times \left(\frac{\text{speed}}{20} + 2 \right)$$

Using d for the distance (in metres) and s for the speed (in kilometres per hour) this statement can be written more shortly as:

$$d = \frac{s}{10} \times \left(\frac{s}{20} + 2 \right)$$

To calculate the overall stopping distance for a speed of 40 km/h write 40 for s in the formula. This gives:

$$d = \frac{40}{10} \times \left(\frac{40}{20} + 2 \right)$$
$$= 4 \times (2 + 2)$$
$$= 4 \times 4$$
$$= 16.$$

To calculate the overall stopping distance for a speed of 80 km/h write 80 for s in the formula. This gives:

$$d = \frac{80}{10} \times \left(\frac{80}{20} + 2 \right)$$
$$= 8 \times (4 + 2)$$
$$= 8 \times 6$$
$$= 48.$$

Check the formula for: (a) 60 km/h   (b) 100 km/h   (c) 120 km/h.

Exercises

Use the formula to find the *overall stopping distance* for a car travelling at: 119

(a) 50 km/h   (b) 90 km/h   (c) 20 km/h   (d) 160 km/h.

Exercises

1. *Roasting times for beef* (at 200°C).

The time for which a joint of beef
should be roasted depends on its mass.
A statement giving the relation between
time in minutes and mass in
kilogrammes is:
$$\text{time} = 40 \times (\text{mass} + \tfrac{1}{2}).$$
Using t for time in minutes,
    m for mass in kilogrammes,
this becomes: $t = 40 \times (w + \tfrac{1}{2})$

Use this formula to find the cooking times (a) in minutes, (b) in hours for a
joint of beef, mass:
        (i) 1 kg (ii) $1\tfrac{1}{2}$ kg (iii) $2\tfrac{1}{2}$ kg (iv) $1\tfrac{1}{4}$ kg (v) 2 kg.

2. *Building a wall*

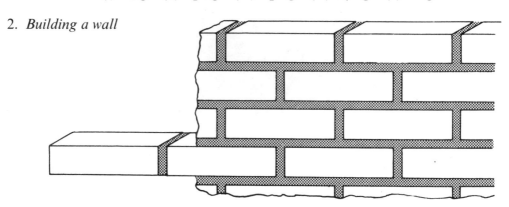

When building a wall, builders adjust the thickness of the mortar joint to
the length and width of the sort of brick they are using.
Here is a statement giving the relation.
    Thickness of mortar joint = length of brick − (2 × width of brick).
Using T for thickness (in centimetres), L for length (in centimetres) and W for
width (in centimetres),
this becomes: $T = L - (2 \times W)$.

In a wall using bricks of length 21·5 cm and width 10·4 cm, what should be
the thickness of the mortar joint?

Take the necessary measurements from a brickwork wall. (You may have to
take an average for each measurement.) Do they agree with the formula?

More formulae

For discussion

Here are some useful formulae.
Look at each in turn and say:
   (a) what the formula is used for; (b) what each letter represents.

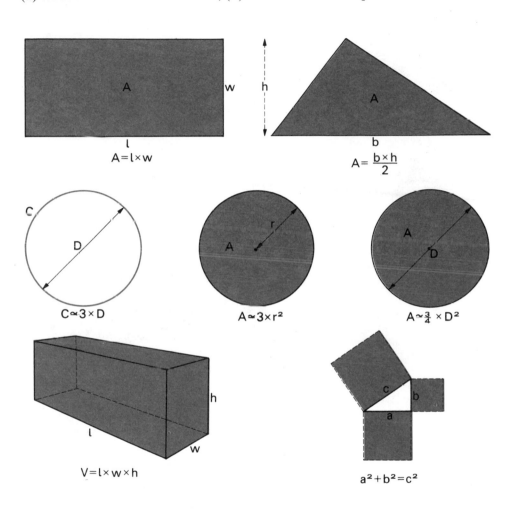

$A = l \times w$

$A = \dfrac{b \times h}{2}$

$C \approx 3 \times D$

$A \approx 3 \times r^2$

$A \approx \tfrac{3}{4} \times D^2$

$V = l \times w \times h$

$a^2 + b^2 = c^2$

Exercises

Select formulae from the list on the previous page and use them to answer the following questions.

1.

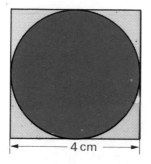
— 4 cm —

Calculate:

(a) the approximate area of the circle;

(b) the area of the square;

(c) the approximate area of the shaded part.

2.

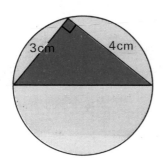
3 cm   4 cm

Calculate:

(a) the length of the diameter of the circle;

(b) the approximate circumference of the circle;

(c) the area of the coloured part.

3. A car travels at an average speed of 56 km/h for $2\frac{1}{2}$ hours. How far has it travelled?

4. Which of the two tanks, A and B, holds most?

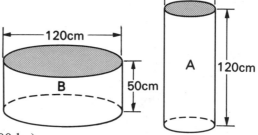

5. The volume of a tonne (1000 kg) of coke is about 3·25 m³. A coal bunker, with a lid, measures 1·8 m by 1·3 m by 1·3 m.

Is it large enough to hold a ton of coke?

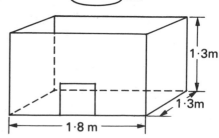

SOME ACTIVITIES

Activity 1

Note and record the dates shown on one hundred pennies. Draw a graph of this information and compare your results with the number of pennies minted in each year. (The number of pennies minted each year can be found in the book *Check Your Change!*)

Activity 2

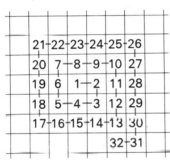

On squared paper write the numbers 1 to 100 in a spiral as shown.

Investigate any number patterns you can see.

Activity 3

Find, as accurately as you can, from how far away people can read the number plate of a car.
(Does the colour of the number plate have any effect?)
Draw a graph of your results.
How many of the people taking part would pass the eyesight test of the Driving Licence Test?

Activity 4

Investigate the use made by pedestrians of a zebra crossing, and the effects on traffic.

Activity 5

An advertisement for car tyres states that 'the area of contact of a car tyre with the ground is the same as that of the sole of a man's shoe', Test the truth of this statement.

Activity 6

  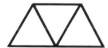 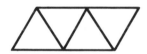

Make these shapes using matchsticks. Make the next two shapes in the sequence.

Investigate sequences formed by:
   (a) the number of triangles in each shape
   (b) the number of parallellograms (including rhombuses) in each shape
   (c) the number of matchsticks in each shape

Activity 7

Find a method of checking the accuracy of a watch.
Use your method to check the accuracy of your own or a friend's watch.

Activity 8

Design a coal bunker to hold one tonne of coke.
Make a scale model of the bunker.

ACKNOWLEDGMENTS

The publishers would like to thank the following for permission to reproduce photographs and figures:

Cambridge Elementary Statistics, Cambridge University Press, page 74;
Camera Press, 58, 114 (bottom right);
J. Allan Cash, 72;
Central Press Photos Ltd, 114 (top right);
G. O. Elam, 114 (bottom left);
Fox Photos, 114 (top left);
Stanley Gibbons Ltd, 18;
Henry Grant, 12, 73;
Keystone Press Agency, 13 (top);
London Transport, 71;
Mansell Collection, 49;
Ministry of Transport, Crown Copyright, 118;
Science Museum, 8;
United Press International, 13 (bottom);
Which? October 1967, by permission of the Consumers Association, 85;
Roger Worsley, 48.
Ordnance Survey, 107, 108, 109;

1:50,000 SCALE (107)
This extract has been produced by the Ordnance Survey from a direct photographic enlargement of the one inch map with appropriate information converted into metric terms. It is not part of any existing series of Ordnance Survey maps. No decisions for metrication of small scale maps had been taken at the date of printing this extract.

1:25,000 SCALE (108)
This extract has been produced by the Ordnance Survey from the 1:25,000 scale Second Series map with appropriate information converted into metric terms. It is not part of any existing series of Ordnance Survey maps. No decisions for metrication of small scale maps had been taken at the date of printing this extract.